Mediterranean

CW01082529

Derived from the Latin for 'in the middle of the lands', the word Mediterranean evokes classicism, cross-fertilisation and blue skies on to which it is only natural to project the idea of some kind of shared identity. However, if a historian's perspective seems to contradict any idea of 'Mediterraneity' – in this volume David Abulafia describes the Mediterranean as a fragmented space, where even in the past a meeting of cultures was the exception in a few cosmopolitan cities rather than the rule – the Muses are drawn to it. The melancholy, reflective vein of the songs described by Turkish musician Zülfü Livaneli and the proverbial conviviality and celebration of free time extolled by Matteo Nucci are viewed with a mixture of fascination and disapproval by Protestant European nations: in an instant, the noble classical profile of *Homo mediterraneus* easily slips into a caricature of laxity and cultural backwardness. However you wish to define it, the Mediterranean seems to be in a state of crisis: neglected by the European Union – which sees the North African and Levantine coasts only as a threat and an energy resource – it is the route of one of the largest migrations in history. While hundreds of millions of holidaymakers flock to its beaches each year, like a distorted image in a fairground mirror, hundreds of thousands of people face a perilous journey in the opposite direction to escape wars, persecution and poverty. The 'liquid road', as Homer described it, grows ever more militarised, congested and polluted, not to mention overheated and overfished. The Romans knew it as *Mare Nostrum* ('Our Sea'), but seen from North Africa it more resembles a wall separating the Arab and European worlds, a source of division rather than a cultural crossroads. It would be wiser to celebrate its variety rather than search for any elusive shared identity, but perhaps 'Mediterraneity' is simply a feeling and as such cares little for rational argument. In spite of everything, however, the Mediterranean still has the power to charm, reassure and console. On its shores modernity has not fully taken root, time passes differently and dialogue between peoples is more common than elsewhere. Perhaps *Homo mediterraneus* has yet to arrive.

1

Other titles in *The Passenger* series

Contents

THE PASSENGER
For explorers of the world
Berlin

THE PASSENGER
For explorers of the world
Paris

THE PASSENGER
For explorers of the world
Rome

THE PASSENGER
For explorers of the world
Ireland

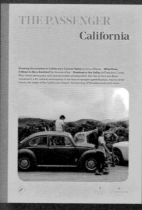

THE PASSENGER
For explorers of the world
California

THE PASSENGER
For explorers of the world
Space

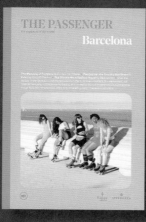

THE PASSENGER
For explorers of the world
Barcelona

THE PASSENGER
For explorers of the world
Nigeria

THE PASSENGER
For explorers of the world
Mexico

Some Numbers

A DEADLY PASSAGE

Recorded migrant deaths by region,
2014–10 May 2022

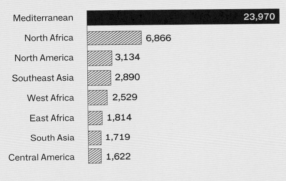

Mediterranean	23,970
North Africa	6,866
North America	3,134
Southeast Asia	2,890
West Africa	2,529
East Africa	1,814
South Asia	1,719
Central America	1,622

SOURCE: MIGRATION DATA PORTAL

RELATIVE DECLINE

Percentage of western
Europe's population living in
the five modern Mediterranean
countries of France, Greece,
Italy, Portugal and Spain in
selected years from 0–1998

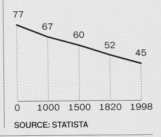

0	1000	1500	1820	1998
77	67	60	52	45

SOURCE: STATISTA

MEDITERRANEAN WARMING

Annual anomalies in air temperature
compared with the decade 1880–9, °C

—— Mediterranean Basin   ------ Planet

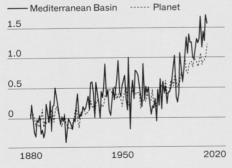

The Mediterranean Basin has warmed
about 1.5°C since pre-industrial times,
20% faster than the global average.

SOURCE: UNITED NATIONS ENVIRONMENT
PROGRAMME (UNEP)

REAL-ESTATE HEAVEN

% of land built over within 150 metres
of the shoreline

▨ 1975   ▬ 2015

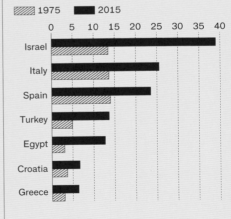

Israel
Italy
Spain
Turkey
Egypt
Croatia
Greece

SOURCE: UNEP

THE MEDITERRANEAN ENDS WHERE THE OLIVE TREE NO LONGER GROWS

The 10 major olive-oil-producing countries, 2023, output in millions of tonnes

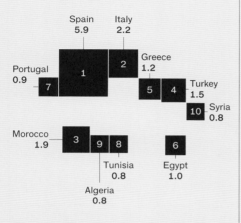

Spain
5.9

Italy
2.2

Portugal
0.9

Greece
1.2

Turkey
1.5

Syria
0.8

Morocco
1.9

Tunisia
0.8

Egypt
1.0

Algeria
0.8

The areas where the olive tree grows cover *c.* 10 million hectares globally, more than 90% of which are in the Mediterranean Basin.

SOURCE: WORLD POPULATION REVIEW

WORLD-BEATING

Largest transport companies, 2022, millions of tonnes

1
MSC
(Switzerland, Italy)
4.8

2
Maersk
(Denmark)
4.1

3
CMA CGM
(France)
3.4

4
COSCO
(China)
2.8

5
Hapag-Lloyd
(Germany)
1.8

SOURCE: WIKIPEDIA

BIODIVERSITY

18%

of the 17,000-plus known marine species live in the Mediterranean, even though the sea represents less than 1% of the ocean surface

SOURCE: UNEP

FISHERMEN

220K

people are employed directly in the Mediterranean fisheries sector (2017), down sharply from 378,000 in 1995

SOURCE: UNION FOR THE MEDITERRANEAN

MARE PLASTICUM

Life cycle of plastic ending up in the Mediterranean, % of the total for each category

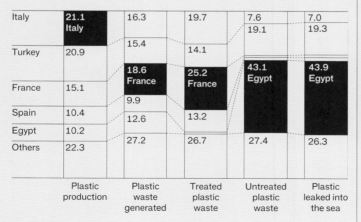

	Plastic production	Plastic waste generated	Treated plastic waste	Untreated plastic waste	Plastic leaked into the sea
Italy	21.1 Italy	16.3	19.7	7.6 / 19.1	7.0 / 19.3
Turkey	20.9	15.4	14.1		
France	15.1	18.6 France	25.2 France	43.1 Egypt	43.9 Egypt
Spain	10.4	9.9	13.2		
Egypt	10.2	12.6			
Others	22.3	27.2	26.7	27.4	26.3

SOURCE: WWF

FAVOURABLE EXCHANGE RATE

Average price (euros) of a double room in a 3-star hotel in selected Mediterranean countries, 2022

Greece	118
Italy	115
France	110
Spain	108
Portugal	98
Tunisia	72
Turkey	68

SOURCE: STATISTA

The Liquid Road

LEÏLA SLIMANI
Translated by Sam Taylor

The Franco-Moroccan writer and journalist Leïla Slimani was the first Moroccan woman to win the Prix Goncourt (2016) with the novel *Chanson douce* (published in English as *The Perfect Nanny* in the USA and *Lullaby* in the UK). In 2017 President Emmanuel Macron appointed her as his personal representative to the Organisation Internationale de la Francophonie, and in 2023 she was chair of the judging panel of the International Booker Prize. Her most recent novel to be published in English is *Watch Us Dance* (2023).

What if the future of freedom were being written in the Maghreb? What if we looked to the other side of the Mediterranean to find the most exciting collective adventures, to discern the outline of a new form of democracy where people questioned violence, economic power and the development of society in a new way?

Between 2011 and 2019 popular uprisings changed the destinies of first Tunisia and then Algeria. I was on Avenue Bourguiba when the Jasmine Revolution began, and I have some extraordinary memories of those moments shared with the Tunisian people. I covered Zine al-Abidine Ben Ali's Tunisia as a journalist from 2008 to 2011, and I had the feeling at the time that this country and its youth were dying. Young people were being driven to illegal emigration and suicide by the nation's ills: police brutality, the economic crisis, endemic corruption and mass unemployment. Tunisia had been undermined so deeply and systematically by its ruling regime that it was hard to see a way out of the situation. In Algeria, similar causes produced comparable effects. And there was a sense of amazement there, too, among observers and the protesters. As the Algerian journalist and author Kamel Daoud put it: 'We had forgotten that we were a people, and in the street we were united once again amid joy and laughter.'

In Europe nobody had forecast the rise of these popular movements because it had been nearly ten years since the European Union had stopped taking an interest in the Maghreb. When I was a student, the Mediterranean was still talked about as a sphere of influence on Europe. Remember Turkey presenting its arguments for joining the club of twenty-seven member states? Even Morocco did not exclude the possibility of gradually joining the union. There's a story that King Hassan II hired teams of Moroccan and Spanish engineers to make a presentation – at a meeting with Jacques Delors, who was president of the European Commission at the time – for his plan to build a bridge that would connect Africa to the Old Continent. In 2008 the French president Nicolas Sarkozy wanted to pursue this dream of bringing together the peoples of the north and south by launching the Union for the Mediterranean, but no stable union could ever be forged with a band of dictators such as Muammar Gaddafi, Bashar al-Assad and Hosni Mubarak.

I am from the Maghreb; I am from the Mediterranean. My attachment to Europe was built across that sea. For me, *Mare Nostrum* was not a border and not yet a cemetery; it was the outline of a community. In Homer the Mediterranean is *hygra*

keleutha, the liquid road, a space of transition and sharing. It is our common heritage. Odysseus made stopovers on the coast of Africa just as he did in the Greek islands. When I first visited Spain, Portugal and Italy I was struck by this feeling of familiarity. So how can we explain Europe's current inability to face that sea? How can we understand the way it has deliberately turned its back on the Mediterranean, when this southward tropism is one of the most fortunate aspects of our continent? We have lost the sea and betrayed that essential part of our identity. How devastating to see the youth of the Maghreb and Africa turning away from the continent that has rejected them and let them down.

The Austrian author Stefan Zweig devoted a large part of his critical work to the European question. In an article published before the Second World War he writes that a Russian exile once told him: 'In the old days, a man had only a body and a soul. Now, he needs a passport too, otherwise he is not treated like a man.' And Zweig, who saw the European continent sink into the horrors of fascism and genocide, adds: 'The first visible manifestation of our century's moral epidemic was xenophobia: the hatred or, at the very least, the fear of the other. Everywhere people defended themselves against the foreigner, they excluded and separated him. All those humiliations that before had been reserved for criminals were now inflicted on travellers.' And still today the question of migration is fundamental, central, because the future of our continent will be decided in terms of our capacity to welcome and also to think about the Other.

*

The European Union, which arose out of the carnage of the Second World War, was intended to be a manifestation of pacifism and the virtues of dialogue. Whether through Schengen or Erasmus, it championed the groundbreaking idea of a future based on reducing borders and encouraging the circulation of people, products and ideas. It is easy to forget this now, but when the European project was first conceived by its founding fathers it was profoundly innovative, even subversive. Turning its back on a warlike, dog-eat-dog vision of the world, the European Union was designed to promote mutual assistance and cooperation. It seems such a sad waste that this democratic ideal is now considered by some to be a sort of outdated, rancid utopianism, while nationalist speeches are cheered and walls are being built on our doorsteps.

But the EU also bears some responsibility for what has happened to it. During the past ten years the union has too often renounced its own moral principles, providing fuel for nationalist and populist arguments. Europe's leaders have demonstrated shameful cynicism by constantly prioritising finance and economics over the construction of a genuine 'European people'. The management of the 2008 economic crisis in Greece constituted the EU's first moral failure: by showing its reactionary side it reduced Europe to a union that was essentially commercial, cold and heartless, embodied by a dominant elite obsessed with profit. Man's indifference to man seemed to become the norm. The second stage in the EU's fall came in 2015 with the migrant crisis. The image of those masses of people fleeing poverty friendship by seeking out what we have in common. The universalism of the Enlightenment must be at the heart of the European project.

It was probably in Europe that the awareness of what is today called 'globalisation' was first forged. Zweig wrote that after the First World War the intellectuals of the Old Continent were both enthusiastic and anxious about the fact that the destiny of different peoples was now so closely linked: 'Humanity, as it spread across the earth, became more intimately interconnected, and today it is shaken by a fever, the entire cosmos shivering with dread.' European integration was driven by that awareness: the great problems of tomorrow will not be resolved at a national scale. Only by combining our efforts will we find solutions to the challenges of the future, and the best example of this is obviously the planet's ecological ultimatum.

It seems to me that Europe must look southwards with interest, respect and passion. It must look to those shores, too, in order to move on to the next chapter in its history; to cease defining itself as an old colonising power and to find strength in its egalitarian values; to stop wallowing in nostalgia and instead pour its energy into inventing a better future. Europe must no longer be defined by Christianity or by exclusive, irreconcilable national identities but must return to the Greek matrix that unites the two sides of *Mare Nostrum*. In Greek the term 'crisis' comes from *krinein*, which means 'to choose'. That's where Europe is now, at a crossroads, and our common future will depend on which path we take next, which moral and philosophical choice we make.

and war and coming up against Europe's haughty indifference left a deep wound in the hearts of many of us. Even today this continent that sees itself as a lighthouse for the world is, in reality, incapable of fighting against the slavery at its doorstep, the death on its shores, the poverty within its borders.

Faced with populists promising simple answers and playing on people's fears, the EU must cast aside its fear of what it is and boldly proclaim that utopia is possible. It must reduce inequality, improve the democratic process, fight climate change and welcome refugees fleeing wars and poverty. To be European is to believe that we are, at once, diverse and united, that the Other is different but equal, that cultures are not irreconcilable, that we are capable of building a dialogue and a

The Sea Between the Lands

DAVID ABULAFIA

Photography by Nick Hannes

A handrail providing disabled access to the sea descends into the water at Izola, Slovenia.

Many politicians, historians and scientists have tried to impose a common identity on the different peoples and civilisations surrounding the Mediterranean – but, in fact, the region's appeal and importance, according to its foremost historian, lie precisely in its fragmentation and variety. This is what has enabled the cultural and commercial exchanges through which some of the region's great inventions – from the Abrahamic religions to mass tourism – continue to exert influence across the world.

13

I

I am often asked to speak in public about two questions concerning the modern Mediterranean, and in this essay I shall interweave them, as they are closely related to one another. The first concerns the way in which the Mediterranean of the 21st century has been moulded by centuries, indeed millennia, of contact between those who have lived on its shores, including its islands, enabling cultural and economic contacts between Europe, Asia and Africa across a long but narrow space. Bearing in mind that the Mediterranean is estimated to contain 0.8 per cent of the maritime surface of the globe, the impact of this small sea on the development of civilisation is out of all proportion to its size and much greater than the impact of other seas that have sometimes been described as 'Mediterraneans', or middle seas, such as the Baltic, the Black Sea or the South China Sea.

The second question concerns the existence of a Mediterranean identity and is connected to the first question through the attempts of various initiatives to create dialogue among all the countries bordering the Mediterranean (which is sometimes extended to include the entire European Union, thereby bringing in countries as far away as Finland). Perhaps the best-known endeavour has been that of French president Nicholas Sarkozy, whose Union pour la Méditerranée, established in 2008, has achieved little even in such vital areas as maritime pollution, let alone cultural interaction. This search for a common identity mirrors in some respects the search for a common European identity that politicians and writers, notably the German philosopher Jürgen Habermas, have pursued. The question Habermas posed is whether such identities exist already or whether they would have to be created. The idea of a Mediterranean identity raises the same problem that arises in Europe about the balance between the local identity of an individual – as a citizen within the Mediterranean region of Italy, for instance – while that individual's country participates in European and Mediterranean initiatives. Clearly, though, there can exist a gap between aspiration and achievement on these fronts. The purpose of this essay is to pursue both questions while keeping in mind the historical perspective.

II

Looking at the first question, we have to confront the fact that the Mediterranean is, and not for the first time, a fractured space politically and economically. Its fractured nature can be traced back over many centuries. Indeed, it was only under the rule of the Roman Empire that the entire Mediterranean fell under a single political authority. This resulted in constant human movement by all manner of people – soldiers, merchants,

DAVID ABULAFIA is Emeritus Professor of Mediterranean History at Cambridge University, where he is a Fellow of Gonville and Caius College. His book *The Great Sea: A Human History of the Mediterranean* has been translated into twelve languages, and *The Boundless Sea: A Human History of the Oceans* won the Wolfson History Prize in 2020. He is a Fellow of the British Academy and Member of the Academia Europaea and was awarded the CBE medal in the King's Birthday Honours, 2023.

NICK HANNES studied photography at the Royal Academy of Fine Arts in Ghent, Belgium. After a number of years working as a photojournalist he decided to focus on long-term documentary projects, in which he tackles socio-political issues with visual metaphors and subtle humour. He has published four books and regularly exhibits in solo and group exhibitions. He has been a recipient of the Magnum Photography Award (2017), the Zeiss Photography Award (2018) and a World Press Photo award (2023).

slaves, bureaucrats, the list is endless – and a high degree of cultural mixing, as well as a certain level of economic integration. There were parts of Rome itself – in areas with a high Jewish population, for example – where you were more likely to hear Greek spoken than Latin. Many factors combined to shatter this unified world – plague, barbarian invasion, internal conflict, perhaps climate change – and what emerged out of it was a fragmented Mediterranean divided mainly among the followers of the Roman Church in the west, the Greek Church in the east and Islam in the south (although that, too, was divided between Sunni and Shia regimes). The fluctuating border between Christians and Muslims – at times running through Spain and to the north of Sicily – provided a platform for cultural contact, although less often for religious interaction. After all, the Latins in the west, the Greeks in the east and the Muslims in the south were all, in different ways, legatees of ancient Greek and Roman culture, so that many important scientific and philosophical texts from antiquity were preserved in Byzantium or the Islamic world, with the Jews often acting as cultural intermediaries, helping with translation work in Spain and elsewhere.

Still, we cannot usefully talk about a common Mediterranean culture or identity during the Middle Ages or subsequent centuries, even allowing for occasional pockets in cities such as Palermo – generally patronised by kings and other powerful individuals – where a meeting of cultures did occur. There were places, it is true, where merchant colonies and the migration of craftsmen and others enabled people from different ethnic and religious backgrounds to live side by side. This was particularly noticeable in the Ottoman Empire, in cities such as Smyrna (Izmir) and Salonika (Thessaloniki), but these were pragmatic relationships concerned more with business than culture. The use of a common Mediterranean language from the 16th to 19th centuries, the so-called Lingua Franca, might appear to point in a different direction, but in reality the language was a patois based on Italian and Spanish with a large number of Turkish and Arabic words, useful in trade and casual everyday contact but not by any means a literary language.

During the 19th century power relationships within the Mediterranean changed dramatically, beginning at the start of the century with the defeat of the Barbary corsairs by the US Navy – the earliest attempt of the newly born United States to make its influence felt overseas – and then the intervention of France in Algeria from 1830 onwards, laying the foundations for an exercise in colonial power that stretched all the way from Ceuta in the west to Alexandria in the east. Not just France but Italy, Great Britain and, on a smaller scale, Spain together gained control of the entire North African shore within less than a hundred years of the French conquest of Algeria. Great Britain became more interested in using the Mediterranean as a channel between the Atlantic and the Indian Ocean, particularly after the opening of the Suez Canal, and Gibraltar, Malta and eventually Cyprus became important bases on this route.

France and Italy, however, had Mediterranean shores of their own. Underlying the French and Italian conquest was an idea of Mediterranean identity, and the aim was in some measure to restore the lost unity of the Roman Mediterranean, reconstituting the *Mare Nostrum* of antiquity. This view found its expression in the thinking and writing of historians and archaeologists at the University of Algiers, a French foundation that was intended to serve the settler population rather than the indigenous Arabs and Berbers. These professors were often respected scholars who made significant contributions to ancient history, but they also saw part of their mission as the justification of French rule through the investigation of the Roman past of what became Algeria. One of their young associates was a historian whose work was to dominate the study of Mediterranean history throughout the second half of the 20th century, Fernand Braudel. I do not want to suggest that Braudel was enthusiastic about French colonialism, but the intellectual environment in which he was working left a deep imprint on his writing, particularly his powerful sense of the fundamental unity of the Mediterranean region.

Ideas of the *Romanitas* of the Mediterranean were expressed even more emphatically in early 20th-century Italy,

FERNAND BRAUDEL (1902–1985)

It was in Algeria, where he had been sent to teach while barely in his twenties, that Fernand Braudel fell under the spell of the sea. In Algiers he discovered the desert and Mediterranean landscapes and started to place geography at the heart of his approach to historiography. Over the following decades his academic career took him to Paris and Brazil, where he began to incorporate the economy into his multidisciplinary approach to history. On the boat that carried him back to Europe in 1937 he met Lucien Febvre, co-founder of the scholarly historical journal *Annales*. Under Febvre's supervision Braudel started work on a thesis that he was later forced to write in a German prison camp without his books and notes, working only from his prodigious memory. The thesis, published in 1949, was *The Mediterranean and the Mediterranean World in the Age of Philip II*, one of the most important historiographical works of the 20th century. It was revolutionary in at least two aspects: the inversion of the object of study (the Mediterranean rather than Philip II) and a new approach to the division of history into periods, making the distinction between the short, medium and long term (*longue durée*), in other words the almost imperceptible fluctuations in the relationships between humanity and our environment. In the first volume of *The Mediterranean*, for example, he describes the tension between inhabitants of the mountains and the plains, with their different cultures and economic models, as a fundamental feature of the history of the Mediterranean over thousands of years.

Top: A holiday resort at La Manga del Mar Menor, a sandbar next to a lagoon in Murcia, Spain. **Bottom:** Russian tourists pose for the camera among the ruins of Hierapolis, near present-day Pamukkale, Turkey.

One sea, two states: boys playing on the beach in Gaza (**top**), while
(**bottom**) people enjoy an afternoon in the sun on the beachfront in Tel Aviv.

'Both the French and the Italians sought to transform the major North African cities into European towns, building handsome new quarters in Tripoli and Algiers that were indistinguishable from the streets of Marseilles or Trieste, even though they stood side by side with ancient medinas and kasbahs.'

beginning with the Italian invasion of Libya in 1911, continuing with the acquisition of the Dodecanese after the First World War and moving up a gear with Mussolini's bid to dominate Mediterranean waters, including the coast of Dalmatia as well as Malta. The cover of an issue of the French magazine *Le Petit Journal* published in October 1911 portrays the arrival of Italian conquerors on the shores of Libya led by a goddess who bears the flame of liberty and whose head is encircled by a halo bearing the word 'CIVILISATION'. Italian warships approach, a symbol of the technological superiority of Europe, while terrified Arabs run away from the immaculately dressed Italian officers whose mere presence is sufficient to win them Tripolitania.

Both the French and the Italians sought to transform the major North African cities into European towns, building handsome new quarters in Tripoli and Algiers that were indistinguishable from the streets of Marseilles or Trieste, even though they stood side by side with ancient medinas and kasbahs. In Tunis, the French constructed one cathedral in the new part of the city and another even grander one in the suburb of Carthage to mark the spot where King Louis IX of France had died while on Crusade in 1270. Unable to furnish a sufficient number of French colonists

in Tunisia and Algeria, the French pursued the great objective of Latinisation by encouraging Italians and Spaniards to settle in town and country; Oran in Algeria contained a larger Spanish population than French – not inappropriately; it had been a Spanish possession during most of the period from 1509 to 1792. And, while Algeria was treated as an integral part of France (different arrangements existed in Morocco and Tunisia), the social and ethnic distinction between Europeans and Arabs remained sharp; only the Jews were considered suitable for Europeanisation and the award of French citizenship.

All this has left a shadow over the Mediterranean that is still present today. Decolonisation was highly desirable for all sorts of reasons, but it created a distance between the newly independent states in North Africa and the Middle East and the former colonial powers, a situation that could be exploited by the Soviet Union, which continued the long Russian tradition of trying to establish bases in the Mediterranean. Having failed to win Greece for communism after the Second World War, the Soviets faced other frustrations within the Mediterranean: the independent-minded policies of Marshal Tito in Yugoslavia and later the alignment of Enver Hoxha's Albania with China put paid to any dreams of infiltrating the Adriatic. On the other hand, the new regimes in Algeria, Egypt and eventually Libya were more sympathetic to the Soviets, seeing them as a source of economic aid, and followed broadly socialist economic policies, although without much evidence of a passion for Marxist theory.

All this was accentuated by the sharp divisions that followed the creation of the State of Israel in 1948. Here again the Soviets at first attempted to win friends in what seemed to be, potentially at least, a socialist society run by egalitarian kibbutzniks, but the lure of close ties with Nasser's Egypt became too strong, and the question of Israel was sucked into the wider question of competition between the Soviet Union and the United States in the Mediterranean. This served only to fragment the Mediterranean even more. It is also vital to recognise that the creation of Israel formed part of a wider pattern of ethnic and religious segregation that had been going on throughout the 20th century. The slaughter and deportation that accompanied the establishment of the Turkish Republic and the expulsion of the Greeks from Asia Minor in 1922, the annihilation by the Germans of 43,000 Jews from Salonika in 1943, the flight of much of the Arab population from what became Israel in 1948, the expulsion of Greeks, Italians and Jews from Egypt in 1956, the hurried departure of the European colonists from Algeria after 1960, not to mention more recent conflicts in Bosnia and Syria, resulted in the emergence of more ethnically homogeneous states around the Mediterranean, but this came at the cost of the disappearance of a rich, interactive urban culture where different communities lived side by side, not without tensions but, by and large, in a degree of harmony.

The image Beirut presents today is of a war-torn city in constant political and economic crisis, no longer the playground of the rich but also no longer the land in which different ethnic and religious groups can live in some sort of harmony. Very few pockets of such peaceful coexistence still exist. In Akko/ Akka, the former Crusader city of Acre, Jewish and Arab Israelis live side by side, although the Old City is mainly Arab, and – despite occasional tensions, even riots – there is an atmosphere of mutual tolerance, whatever the political preferences of either side. Perhaps the best example of continuing harmony is to be found in what is, paradoxically, the last colony in the Mediterranean, Gibraltar, where Christians, Jews, Muslims and Hindus live alongside one another without obvious friction. That is a community of roughly 50,000 people. If we compare it to modern Alexandria, we see how a very large city that a hundred years ago hosted a mixed population of Italians, Greeks, Jews, Turks, Copts, Maltese as well as Muslim Egyptians has become a monochrome city, which, apart from a sizeable Coptic population that tries to stay below the radar, is almost entirely Sunni Muslim and Arab. Homogeneity may have its social advantages, but they are surely outweighed by the disadvantages.

III

A further factor that has accentuated the fragmentation of the Mediterranean is the way that the European Union has evolved. European countries that are still excluded aspire to membership and to achieving the high standard of living that the member states have reached – often, as in the cases of Portugal or Lithuania, from a low starting point.

THE PASSENGER David Abulafia

DRAINING THE SEA

Immediately after the First World War the German architect Herman Sörgel threw himself into a visionary project that promised to resolve European economic problems and prevent a repeat of the tensions that had led to the conflict. His utopian plan called for the construction of a thirty-five-kilometre dam, three hundred metres in height and three kilometres wide, near Gibraltar to close off the Mediterranean. Then by building a similar dam in the Dardanelles, it would have been possible to close off the circulation of water and trigger a drastic lowering of the Mediterranean through evaporation. The vast tracts of land that would have been delivered, according to Sörgel's geopolitical reasoning, would have driven European and African cooperation, reduced the need for the colonial powers to search for a place in the sun and resolved any dependence on oil and coal once and for all, since the vast quantity of energy supplied by the dams would have rendered fossil fuels superfluous. Europe and Africa would have merged into the supercontinent of Atlantropa, a bridge between Tunisia and Sicily would have paved the way for a rail link between Cape Town and Berlin and the riches of Africa would have been brought within European reach. After more than twenty years of discussions, the project, which was disliked by the Nazis because of its pacifist motivation, was buried along with its architect in 1952. This would not have been the first closure of the Strait of Gibraltar, however; the Mediterranean has gone through cyclical phases of drought and flood, with the last drying event occurring six million years ago.

That wish to become a member is true not just at the state level – witness the ambitions of Albania and other Balkan states to be admitted – but at the individual level, among migrants (more of which later). At the state level the governments of Mediterranean members of the EU have tended to look northwards, away from the Mediterranean, towards Brussels, Frankfurt and other centres of political and economic power in northern Europe. Indeed, when Greece faced severe economic crisis Berlin was able to determine the direction its government should take. Politicians have to choose priorities, and in doing so they bear in mind the fact that, in a democracy, the public will not forgive them for failing to capitalise on the best advantages. So their neglect of opportunities to invest on the massive scale that is needed in countries such as Tunisia has accentuated the sense of a Mediterranean divide. It has also given other countries, notably China, the opportunity to further their interests both in the countries the member states have neglected – once again Tunisia springs to mind – as well as in what some EU states regard as disposable assets, such as the port of Piraeus, in which China has invested heavily (see 'Piraeus Speaks Chinese' on page 166).

Most notably, no one has any idea how to address the issue of trans-Mediterranean migration. This has become increasingly problematic, not just because of civil war in Syria and conflicts in Iraq and Afghanistan but because the stream of migrants coming out of sub-Saharan Africa shows no sign of diminishing. Infant mortality has plunged in countries such as Nigeria, which is unquestionably good news, but, even with the enormous economic improvements there over the last thirty

Above: The Strait of Gibraltar seen from the Spanish North African enclave of Ceuta.
Right: A makeshift ticket office at an amusement park in Budva, Montenegro.
Opposite: A Catholic procession in La Línea de la Concepción, the Andalusian town that borders Gibraltar (**top**); children playing in Beit Lahia in the Gaza Strip (**bottom**).

The Sea Between the Lands

'The one area in which the economy of the Mediterranean has experienced an unprecedented boom during the post-war period is tourism, along with the opportunities that has created for employment.'

years or more, there are not enough jobs for a vastly inflated population. And not just vastly inflated, vastly better educated – young men, very often English speaking, have high expectations that can only be met by making a gruelling journey across the Sahara Desert, perhaps then across the Atlas Mountains, in the hope of breaking into the Spanish enclaves on the northern shore of Morocco: Ceuta and Melilla.

Since the final years of the 20th century migration has become one of the characteristic features of the Mediterranean. We have before our eyes the image of people setting out in flimsy inflatable boats, often without lifejackets, carrying their children – whether from the Aegean coast of Turkey to the Greek islands, or from Libya to Malta, or from Morocco to Spain. Although the methods employed to enter the lands of the European Union are new, the phenomenon itself is not, but in the past much of it was actually contained within particular countries. The history of migration out of Sicily and southern Italy began as far back as the late 19th century and was largely directed towards North or South America but also, as has been seen, towards Tunisia and then towards the new Italian colony of Libya. In the 1950s and 1960s it was redirected to the towns of northern Italy. Southern Italian agriculture, already suffering from neglect and lack of investment, declined still further as villages were abandoned. By contrast, many of the African or Asian migrants who reached the Mediterranean in the years either side of 2000 aimed simply to set foot on European soil and then to head northwards to France, Germany, the UK or Sweden, but it is the Mediterranean members of the European Union who have had to deal with the influx in the first instance. At the same time there is the old reality of migration. As living standards have improved in western Europe, menial tasks have been offloaded on to the migrants, who can find employment in hotels as chambermaids, waiters, cleaners and construction workers – for the one area in which the economy of the Mediterranean has experienced an unprecedented boom during the post-war period is tourism, along with the opportunities that has created for employment.

IV

In the second half of the 20th century the Mediterranean, no longer a vital seat of commercial or naval power, found a new vocation: mass tourism. Mass tourism first took off in the Mediterranean, and the region attracts around 400 million visitors each year. This southward migration has had serious environmental consequences, placing heavy demands on limited water and energy supplies (notably in

Cyprus) and replacing sweeping vistas of coasts and hillsides with poorly designed, monotonous blocks of white concrete houses (notably in Spain). What changed dramatically in the late 20th century was the number and aims of the visitors and the ease with which they could reach most corners of the Mediterranean. Tourists replaced travellers. The real transformation occurred with the arrival of the aeroplane. Cheap, safe, rapid air travel took time to arrive. Between 1960 and 1973 the number of annual visitors to Majorca rose precipitously from 600,000 to 3.6 million, and, by the start of the 21st century, tourism accounted for 84 per cent of the Majorcan economy. Whole concrete towns, such as Palma Nova, were created to serve the tourist industry. No country could compete with Spain, which was exactly what the Franco regime wanted. In 1959 a new Stabilisation Plan for the Spanish economy envisaged the rapid expansion of tourism in Mediterranean Spain, the Balearics and the Canaries. This was seen as a way of making Franco's Spain respectable while the horrors of its recent history were conveniently ignored. Along the coast of Spain vast swathes of concrete brought a degree of prosperity but also showed little consideration for the natural beauty of the Costa Brava and the rest of Spain's Mediterranean coast.

All of this shows how persistently

FLOATING CITIES

As well as mass tourism, the Mediterranean also attracts those from the opposite end of the economic spectrum. Tourism as practised by the super-rich tends to be less visible, but to regular families on their excursions it manifests itself in the form of the enormous yachts anchored at luxury marinas in the Mediterranean's most exclusive and picturesque little ports. There are almost six thousand superyachts (ranging from thirty to 180 metres in length) around the world, and numbers are increasing at the rate of a few hundred a year. According to one estimate half this fleet spends eight of the twelve months of the year in the Mediterranean, and each summer a third of them flock to the Côte d'Azur. After the Russian invasion of Ukraine, when the governments in a number of European countries moved to seize the property of Russian oligarchs close to the Kremlin, there was a rush to the safer harbours of Turkey and Dubai. The few confiscated yachts ended up in a legal limbo, with the authorities attempting to navigate their way through the maze of shell companies used to conceal the identity of their real owners and governments footing the bills for the exorbitant maintenance costs. It almost goes without saying that superyachts are harmful to the environment, like other large boats including ferries and cargo ships, causing marine and noise pollution and releasing heavy metals into the water, but the problems they cause are amplified by their numbers and concentration, particularly during the summer months, and the fact that they sail and moor much closer to the coast, where their immense anchors can destroy sections of the seabed.

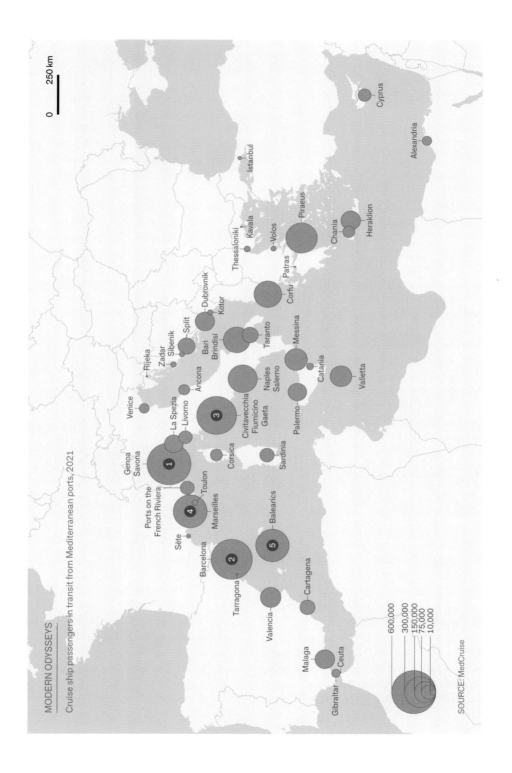

MODERN ODYSSEYS

Cruise ship passengers in transit from Mediterranean ports, 2021

0 — 250 km

Istanbul

Cyprus

Alexandria

Piraeus
Thessaloniki
Kavala
Volos
Chania
Heraklion
Patras
Corfu

Dubrovnik
Kotor
Split
Sibenik
Zadar
Rijeka
Bari
Brindisi
Taranto
Messina
Catania
Valletta
Venice
Ancona
La Spezia
Livorno
Naples
Salerno
Civitavecchia
Fiumicino
Gaeta
Palermo
Genoa
Savona
Corsica
Sardinia
Ports on the
French Riviera
Toulon
Marseilles
Sète
Balearics
Barcelona
Tarragona
Cartagena
Valencia
Malaga
Ceuta
Gibraltar

1
2
3
4
5

600,000
300,000
150,000
75,000
10,000

SOURCE: MedCruise

26   THE PASSENGER   David Abulafia

The Mediterranean attracts around one-third of all global tourism and is the world's premier tourist destination, with more than 400 million international arrivals in 2019

The taste of salt

International tourist arrivals in the Mediterranean region, 1995–2019, millions

- Southwestern Mediterranean: Morocco, Algeria, Tunisia, Libya
- **Northeastern Mediterranean:** Slovenia, Croatia, Bosnia and Herzegovina, Montenegro, Albania, Greece
- **Southeastern Mediterranean:** Egypt, Israel, Palestine, Lebanon, Syria, Turkey, Cyprus
- **Northwestern Mediterranean:** Spain, France, Italy, Monaco, Malta

Tourism dependence

Impact of tourism (direct, indirect and induced) on the economies of countries in the Mediterranean region before and during Covid as a % of GDP

2019   2020

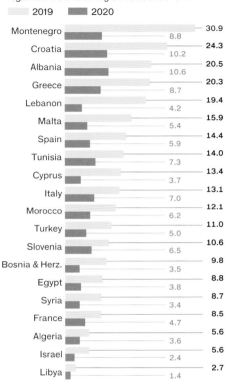

Country	2019	2020
Montenegro	30.9	8.8
Croatia	24.3	10.2
Albania	20.5	10.6
Greece	20.3	8.7
Lebanon	19.4	4.2
Malta	15.9	5.4
Spain	14.4	5.9
Tunisia	14.0	7.3
Cyprus	13.4	3.7
Italy	13.1	7.0
Morocco	12.1	6.2
Turkey	11.0	5.0
Slovenia	10.6	6.5
Bosnia & Herz.	9.8	3.5
Egypt	8.8	3.8
Syria	8.7	3.4
France	8.5	4.7
Algeria	5.6	3.6
Israel	5.6	2.4
Libya	2.7	1.4

SOURCE: PLAN BLEU 2022, INTERREG MED, EUROPEAN INSTITUTE OF THE MEDITERRANEAN (IEMED)

demand for sun, sea and sand has brought northern Europeans in particular to the Mediterranean. In some places marked cultural differences between the native population and tourists have created difficulties (for instance, over the exposure of more and more flesh in public); in addition, demand for familiar foods, including fast foods and even British fish and chips, have eroded the culinary traditions of certain regions. But bikini tourism, as it can appropriately be called, is only part of the picture. Visitors have also seized the opportunity to see the wonders of Italy, Spain and elsewhere; a day trip from the coast to Pisa or Granada has also become part of the experience. And alongside mass tourism interest in historical sites has flourished, further boosted by the arrival

THE PASSENGER   David Abulafia

'The interest of the Mediterranean lies in its variety, its disunity, not in the supposed unity on which those politicians, historians and social scientists have insisted.'

of American, Japanese and (at least until the pandemic) Chinese tourists in the region. It may appear rude and arrogant to refer to this phenomenon, too, as a pollutant, but packed streets, museums outside which long queues form and overrun archaeological sites have all become a standard experience for the Mediterranean traveller.

That so many people want to see archaeological treasures in Delphi or Olympia or works of art in Venice or Florence is part of a welcome process of the democratisation of culture. At the same time the presence of large crowds often makes these very objects and places harder to understand and appreciate. All this is further complicated by the expansion of the cruise industry within and well beyond the Mediterranean. When two thousand people arrive on a ship in the harbour at Dubrovnik the result is traffic jams not of cars but of people in the narrow passageways of a UNESCO World Heritage Site; and the Mediterranean has more of these than any other corner of the globe, with Italy and then Spain in the lead. The length of time it has taken for cruise ships to be banned from entering the Venetian lagoon has also had serious environmental consequences and suggests that profit comes first in the eyes of the authorities. The decision to charge an entry fee to deter day-trippers from coming into Venice may reduce numbers, or it may simply turn into a money-spinner, like the daily taxes often added to a hotel bill in several European cities.

These developments have great significance for the problem of a Mediterranean identity. Mass tourism has undermined culinary traditions, but culinary traditions also indicate that one should not speak too rapidly about a common identity. A tray of *tapas* in Spain will carry very different foods to a tray of *meze* in Cyprus. Wine production is low in Islamic countries but very high (and of high quality) in France, Italy and Spain. Family structures differ, as do social attitudes and literary, artistic and musical traditions, not to mention religious outlooks, tolerance of political corruption, languages spoken and much else besides. The interest of the Mediterranean lies in its variety, its disunity, not in the supposed unity on which those politicians, historians and social scientists have insisted. When one talks of a Mediterranean identity, common features become reduced to vague and somewhat condescending comments, such as the assumption that people who live in Mediterranean lands are not very punctual, or that they are noisy and excitable, or don't display the outwardly unfriendly reserve found among Finns, Swedes and other inhabitants of the far north. These caricatures, even were they valid, would not add up to a common Mediterranean identity.

V

That does not mean people of the Mediterranean lack shared concerns of enormous importance. The search for greater stability within the Mediterranean has increasingly turned away from political rivalries towards ecological issues that can only be addressed if all the nations of the region agree to transcend political differences and to work together. The centre of gravity in Europe still lies in the north, despite the accession to the EU of a few more Mediterranean countries (all small) at the start of the 21st century. This confirms the impression that the Mediterranean has lost its place at the centre of the Western world, a process that began as early as 1492 when new opportunities across the Atlantic beckoned, and early in the 21st century it seems that the great economic powerhouse of the future will be China. In the worldwide economy of the present century, an integrated Mediterranean has local rather than global significance. The Mediterranean has ceased to function as a meeting place of civilisations and as home to a tight network of economic bonds. Seas both join and divide, sometimes more one than the other. This sea that has so often joined three continents is now a frontier dividing the continents from one another. And yet its powerful historical heritage still places it at the centre of the world when we look at cultural developments across the centuries. To say this is not to disparage the civilisations of northern Europe, nor of China, Japan and elsewhere. The Mediterranean has seen the birth of two of the Abrahamic religions, Judaism and Christianity, and the

Top: Tourists in pole position for the Monaco Grand Prix.
Bottom: A water tower destroyed by NATO bombing in Sirte, Libya.

A SEA OF PROBLEMS

Historically the topography of the Mediterranean was central to the development of trade and growth of civilisations, but now that its waters are ever more polluted the semi-enclosed geography of the basin is aggravating its environmental issues. Seawater only circulates via the Strait of Gibraltar, and it takes between eighty and a hundred years for the waters of the Mediterranean to change completely. If we think about how much we have polluted the sea in recent decades, at these rates it risks turning into one big sewer. Among the factors that make it one of the world's dirtiest seas are tourism and population density, not to forget the pollution from industrial and agricultural effluents from rivers such as the Nile, the Rhône and the Po. Although it covers less than 1 per cent of the world's marine surface area, it is affected by 20 per cent of oil-industry pollution. Crossed every day by three hundred oil tankers, the Mediterranean boasts the highest concentration of tar in the world. Shipping, in particular cruise ships, has a devastating impact, not just on water pollution but also on air quality. And then there's noise pollution. While 3.8 per cent of the Mediterranean was affected in 2005, eight years later this had grown to 27 per cent. Sea creatures are not the only ones impacted by the din of human activities; one recent study showed that *Posidonia oceanica*, a plant vitally important to the ecosystem, is also distressed by just two hours of exposure to low-frequency noise.

rise to great power of the third, Islam. It has been the birthplace of Greek philosophy and of Roman law, which still leave deep imprints on civilisations across the world. What has been suggested here is that its cultural riches do need some protection. Somehow they have to be made available to everyone but at the same time must be protected from overexposure and deterioration, Venice being an especially important case.

Meanwhile, as the years have gone by, maritime pollution has become a more urgent problem, with the effects of climate change increasingly visible in higher temperatures, forest fires and desiccation; fish stocks are at risk as plastic pellets are ingested by sea creatures and overfishing threatens sustainability. Initiatives to clean the sea and to protect the monuments and artefacts are subjects for action as well as discussion, and the failure to take decisive action at a time when climate change may well transform the physical environment throughout the Mediterranean leaves less room for optimism about the future than one would wish.

The Mediterranean has had a brilliant past, and it deserves to have a brilliant future as well. 🐦

The Sea Between the Lands

Shipwreck

ANNALISA CAMILLI
Translated by Eleanor Chapman
Photography by André Liohn

An eleven-year-old boy from Guinea looks towards Catania, Sicily, through a porthole of the Médecins Sans Frontières vessel *Aquarius*, which patrolled the waters between Libya and Italy before it was seized by the Italian authorities.

In March 2023 a severely overcrowded boat sank in what is supposedly the Libyan search-and-rescue zone – yet another example of the North African country's inability to offer any real aid to migrants but also one of Europe's complicity in the tragedies taking place at sea as it strives to offload any kind of responsibility.

35

W ater in his throat, his companions screaming, frozen hands.

Images from the wreck churn in his mind, keeping him from sleep. He saw his fellow travellers drown. Many of them couldn't swim, and when the boat capsized they slipped to the bottom of the ocean, disappearing.

Siful is thirty-three years old and is one of seventeen survivors of a shipwreck that took place on 11 March 2023, a hundred nautical miles north of Benghazi, Libya. He had left Tobruk the previous day along with forty-six others, all men between eighteen and forty-seven. After a few hours the boat's engine broke down.

A bewildered look in his eyes, a tuft of black hair over his forehead, he is now in hospital in Sicily. These images flick through his mind like clips from a film: the stormy sea, the traffickers prodding them with guns to force them on to a boat just eight metres long in the middle of winter.

The line of the shore behind them, and then the huge, ever-growing waves, the stomach-ache, the nausea, the fear, the vomit, the stench of diesel, the cold, the waves washing over them, water getting in, phoning the emergency number, boats on the horizon, his companions' screams, their tears and finally the tumbling, capsizing, salt, freezing water, grasping on to the boat, the pain in his leg.

He takes a sheet of paper and draws the boat with people on board. Then he writes his name: Siful. He wants to let his family in Bangladesh know that he's alive. After falling overboard he was rescued by a cargo ship, the *Froland*, then taken to Pozzallo in Italy and admitted to hospital in Modica with a fractured leg. It hurts, but the pain reminds him that he is still alive. He could have been among the dead, but instead he is with the living.

Luckily, he can swim. He forced his legs against the waves so as not to sink, clung to the hull of the capsized boat and thrashed about while those who couldn't swim clung to him. Now their arms, their cries for help, torment him.

'A few hours after leaving the Libyan coast the sea was getting rougher and rougher. Some people wanted to turn back. We were crammed together. It was very cold, and the waves made me feel sick. The cold was unbearable. When traffickers made us board, they told us there would be water and food on the boat, but it wasn't true,' he recalls. Then the boat capsized. 'Everyone was shouting and calling for help. I clung to the wreckage with the force of desperation, but many didn't know how to swim, and I saw them disappear beneath the waves. We were trying to encourage each other: someone will come to save us.'

The journey had been planned for a while. Siful had paid a thousand US dollars for a flight from Bangladesh to

ANNALISA CAMILLI is an Italian investigative journalist. Since 2007 she has been covering Italian current affairs for *Internazionale*, with a particular focus on immigration. In 2017 she won the Anna Lindh Foundation award for the article 'La barca senza nome' ('The Boat with No Name'), and in 2019 Rizzoli published her book *La legge del mare: Cronache dei soccorsi nel Mediterraneo* ('The Law of the Sea: Chronicles of Relief Efforts in the Mediterranean').

ANDRÉ LIOHN is a photographer, film producer and documentary filmmaker. During the Libyan Civil War he documented the work of frontline doctors for the International Committee of the American Red Cross. He has won the Robert Capa Gold Medal, an award from the National Press Photographers Association and many others. With other award-winning photographers he was one of the creators of the project ADIL – Almost Dawn in Libya: Photojournalism as a Possible Bridge for Reconciliation. His photos and videos have been published in major international newspapers.

Benghazi; he paid a trafficker from his country to arrange it all. He had worked as a carpenter in Bangladesh, but he had always wanted to go to Europe. In Libya he had been shut in a safe house, an apartment with other Bangladeshi nationals preparing to leave. They waited for a few weeks, and then they were loaded into vans and taken to the shore. When he saw the boat, how small it was, he had second thoughts. He no longer wanted to leave, but the Libyans forced them all on board, threatening them with weapons.

They set sail, but after a few hours the engine stopped. For three days the little wooden boat was adrift in the middle of the Mediterranean. Then it sank.

ADRIFT

It's Friday night, and the Alarm Phone group, a European network of volunteers monitoring the central Mediterranean, is gathered in an apartment in Marseilles. Among them are several of the founding members of the organisation, which has cells active across Europe and North Africa. They are radical activists of a wide range of ages. They refer to each other by aliases or by the name of the city where they are based in order to remain anonymous. They monitor the Mediterranean, reporting deaths at sea and denouncing the consequences of Europe's closed-border policies.

During the night of 10/11 March the Marseilles group received six phone calls, all from Sfax in Tunisia. The voices on the phone were family members of people on board small boats or fishermen calling to alert the volunteers and to ask them to call the rescue services. In the first few months of 2023 the Tunisian route became the primary one for migrants crossing the Mediterranean to reach Italy by boat, in part because of Tunisia's extremely precarious economic and political situation. According to data from the Italian Ministry of the Interior, between the beginning of 2023 and 13 March of that year 12,083 people arrived in Italy from Tunisia. In the same period only 7,057 people chose the once pre-eminent Libyan route. The points of departure have also changed in Libya, with increasing numbers of people choosing to set sail from the much more distant ports of Tobruk or Derna in Cyrenaica.

Mariam (a fake name to protect her identity) looks at her phone. It's 1 a.m. While the other volunteers in the group scrutinise the computer screen and carry on their discussion, Mariam lies down on the sofa and falls asleep. But soon, at 1.32, she is awoken. The phone is ringing again.

'Please, help us!' they scream down the line. She can hear people crying, a lot of commotion in the background. Mariam calmly explains that they need to let her know their coordinates, which they can check on a satellite phone. But the call drops. Silence.

Five minutes later the phone rings again. The signal is bad. A man's voice reads out some numbers – the boat's position. He is calmer. He first says the numbers rapidly and then repeats them more slowly.

33°55′N, 18°27′E.

Mariam repeats the coordinates back to him to make sure they are correct then types them into the Watch the Med website to find out where they're calling from.

It brings up a pinprick in the middle of the sea, northwest of Benghazi in the Libyan search-and-rescue (SAR) zone, twenty nautical miles south of the Maltese SAR zone. It's something of a black hole as regards rescue services.

Mariam asks for confirmation of the coordinates, but the line keeps breaking up. In the background she can hear the anxious shouts of the people on board. Mariam calls back while the others start to set processes in motion. For half an hour no one answers. Then, at 2 a.m., someone picks up the phone again. The boat has drifted a small distance. There is a strong wind, the signal is bad, the line keeps breaking up.

Mariam thinks how scared they must be on board, their cries. The others are writing an email to the Italian coastguard, copying in their Maltese and Libyan colleagues.

It is 2.28 a.m.

There is no reply from the Italians or Maltese. A volunteer checks the ship-tracking apps MarineTraffic and VesselFinder for civilian ships in that stretch of sea. The apps do not track military ships. A tanker, the *Amax Avenue*, is in the area. Why don't the competent authorities command it to go immedi-

ately to the boat's rescue? she wonders. They would have previously. She has a lot of experience with this sort of operation, but every time feels like the first.

She sets about trying to find a phone number for the ship's owner, wanting to alert the captain of the tanker directly, but she can't find one.

At 3 a.m. they call the tanker's insurance company. The man who answers doesn't seem to be interested in contacting the captain and alerting him to the danger faced by the people on that little boat. 'It's the maritime authorities who have to alert the captain. I can't do it,' the man says.

The volunteers tell him it's urgent, there's a boat in distress. They copy him into the emails they're sending to the coastguard.

'I'll go and read your email, but I don't think I'm in a position to help,' the man says before hanging up.

There's another ship in the area, the *Gamma Star*, but not one of the boats nearby changes course towards the people in distress.

An hour later, at 4.30, they contact another insurance company.

This time a very nice man answers the call. At first he says he will try to help them, but then he checks his email. 'I'm sorry, there's nothing I can do.'

Mariam is shattered. She is about to hand the case over to another group of volunteers, but she can't tear herself away. At 6.40 a.m. the boat calls again.

A MIGRANT CEMETERY

In Zarzis, Tunisia, bodies of migrants are found on the beach almost every day. Close to the border with Libya, the town has experienced huge difficulties in dealing with this and has often failed to treat the bodies that are discovered with humanity. That was until Rachid Koraïchi, an Algerian artist with family ties to Tunisia, intervened, designing and creating the Jardin d'Afrique, a cemetery that looks more like a palace, to give the victims an appropriate burial, regardless of their religion. The inauguration in June 2021 was attended by a bishop, an imam and a rabbi. It is impossible to identify all the dead, but Koraïchi's efforts, in combination with those of the Red Crescent in Zarzis, have led to the creation of an association that is establishing a DNA database of everyone who is buried so they can one day be identified by their families. He is not the only artist in the town to have created a memorial for the *harraga*, those who burn their documents before leaving in the hope of entering Europe. Mohsen Lihidheb has been doing the same thing for years, collecting the objects returned by the sea in his *Mémoire de la mer* – items such as shoes, clothes and bottles, some containing messages to which he has tried to respond. He also crowdfunded the creation of a cemetery and is in contact with his counterpart in Sicily where, on the island of Lampedusa, a section of the cemetery is devoted to those who have died at sea, and where, too, a DNA bank of the drowned was set up after the Mediterranean claimed the lives of 368 people off the island's coast on 3 October 2013.

She asks once more for their coordinates. They're more or less in the same place.

33°53′N, 18°38′E

The shift finishes at 7 a.m. The case passes to a team made up of another volunteer in Marseilles and two others in Hanau, Germany.

The people on the boat ask if there is anyone who understands Bengali. They are all Bangladeshis on board. There are around fifty of them. Some of them speak Arabic, others basic English.

Communication is difficult. The man on the phone speaks quickly. He can say just two words in English: 'Sister, come.'

It is 9.30 in the morning, and a bright light is shining through the window of the Hanau apartment where alarm calls are ringing. The voices on the phone are desperate, the man on the boat is crying. 'We have no more food or water,' he says in English. 'There is no more fuel, the engine is broken, the boat is broken,' he shouts again.

They can hear screams in the background. There is someone who speaks Arabic. They ask him to confirm the coordinates again. On the boat they get angry. 'Why do you keep asking us the same thing? Why don't you come to save us?'

The call drops. An Alarm Phone volunteer tries to call Tripoli; the coastguard usually replies after several attempts. He dials the number, but it rings into the void. No one answers.

It is already Saturday. The sixty-two-year-old man heats up some water for coffee then sits back down at the computer to write another email to the Italian and Maltese coastguards. 'There are forty-seven people in danger, they're drifting.'

'It's definitely them; the boat is packed. The people look like tiny, distant specks, waving their arms. There are about fifty of them at the mercy of the sea.'

MAYDAY

The small, white, twin-engined aeroplane takes off from Lampedusa as the sun rises in the east and the still-cold March light creeps up the flat, grey runway into the sea. It is crewed by five young Germans, all of them wearing orange overalls. They are all highly experienced in sea rescue, many of them having started this work around the Greek islands during the refugee crisis of 2015.

It will take a couple of hours for the *Seabird 2*, an aircraft operated by the German NGO Sea-Watch, to reach the boat in distress. Having been alerted by Alarm Phone they are flying towards the boat to try to view it from above and get an idea of what is going on. If things are going badly they will see it being intercepted by the so-called Libyan coastguard; if things go well – as they hope – a cargo ship will try to rescue the people on board. The worst-case scenario, in reality, is that they won't find the boat at all if it sinks during the time it takes them to get there.

The sea is rough. They see the water surging beneath them, white foam frothing on the waves. The radio is transmitting constant updates on the weather conditions.

When they come into proximity of the 'target', as it's described in technical terms, they look through the windows with binoculars, searching for any sign of the boat on the dark sea. One of them spots something and exclaims, 'There!' It is a dot on the waves.

The aeroplane draws closer. It's 10.34 a.m. It's definitely them; the boat is packed. The people look like tiny, distant specks, waving their arms. There are about fifty of them at the mercy of the sea.

The boat is grey, rectangular, made out of wood.

'Mayday relay, mayday,' the pilot says into the radio transmitter in his hand. 'A grey wooden boat with fifty people on board, stationary in high waves, people in distress, immediate assistance is required,' he continues, broadcasting the distress call to all boats in the area. Fifty people in a boat, fifty people in the waves, fifty people in danger.

Three minutes later a ship sailing under the flag of the Marshall Islands, the *Basilis L*, answers the call. The captain is a man who speaks faltering English with a marked Greek accent. He says that he is twenty nautical miles away from the boat in distress and that he wants to make towards it.

The ship left Slovenia a few days ago, stopped off in Cyprus and is on its way to Libya. A little later, from the aeroplane they make another call to the captain of the *Basilis L*. The ship is getting closer; it's fifteen nautical miles away, but the Italian coastguard coordination centre in Rome has ordered it to follow Libya's lead. 'They advised me to follow Libyan coastguard. These were their instructions,' the man on the bridge of the ship tells them before hanging up.

He must monitor the boat until the Libyans intervene. These are the instructions from the Italian authorities.

MIGRATION ROUTES

Schengen Area

Eastern Mediterranean route

Central Mediterranean route

Eastern African route

Western African route

○ Principal migration hubs

● Transit cities

⬚ Arrivals by land and sea, 2022

Bulgaria
16,767

Istanbul

TURKEY

Cyprus
17,284

Cairo

EGYPT

Athens

Greece
18,775

GERMANY

AUSTRIA

FRANCE

Paris

Rome

Italy
105,131

Malta
444

Tunis

Tripoli

LIBYA

TUNISIA

Ouargla

ALGERIA

Algiers

Spain
(coast and Balearics)
13,248

Spain
24,404

Madrid

Mahdia

Oujda

MOROCCO

Spain
(Ceuta and Melilla)
2,289

Rabat

0   250 km

SOURCE: Reuters, International Organization for Migration

They can see the *Basilis L* from the aeroplane. It's a long, low, black-and-red ship, moving slowly, carrying chemical products and petroleum derivatives. From the ground the Sea-Watch team tries to contact the Libyan coastguard. After several failed attempts someone in Tripoli answers the phone. The Libyan authorities are aware of the case and say that they have relayed the information to the coordination centre in Benghazi. But everyone knows there are no relations between Tripoli and Benghazi. During the Libyan Civil War Benghazi was an Islamist-militia stronghold, and since 2017 it has been controlled by gangs close to Khalifa Haftar, the general who governs Cyrenaica and does not recognise the government in Tripoli. Before the 2011 revolution the city had been a bastion of opposition to Muammar Gaddafi.

The crew of the *Seabird 2* asks Tripoli if Benghazi is launching a rescue mission. The Libyan authorities reply that they are not currently doing so.

'Sir, can you please tell me what patrol vessels you are sending?' a volunteer asks down the line.

'We are trying to send them, we are trying,' the man from Tripoli replies awkwardly.

'Do you not have patrol vessels in Benghazi?' the woman asks again.

'We do not have patrol vessels to send,' Tripoli says hesitatingly.

The tension in the plane is palpable. It is not easy to watch the boat in distress below, knowing that there is no one in a position to intervene.

The *Basilis L* is 0.8 nautical miles from the drifting boat. From the plane they make another call to the captain, telling him that there are no patrol vessels coming from Tripoli or from Benghazi. But the captain of the ship replies that they have to wait for the Libyans to arrive, that they cannot intervene because of the bad weather.

At 1.26 p.m. the *Seabird 2* leaves the area. It is short on fuel and has to return. They make a last call to the Italian coordination centre. 'No one is intervening. The Libyans have no boats to send.'

'OK, thanks, bye,' Rome replies.

Twelve hours have passed since the first call for help. It is only at around 6.40 p.m. on 11 March that the Italian coastguard in Rome starts to coordinate a rescue mission.

WRECKED

He is freezing to death. The boy in front of him has passed out after vomiting. The aeroplane that was circling above them has gone. There is a boat on the horizon, looking like a low, grey cloud or sometimes like the outline of a whale. Every now and again it seems like it's getting closer; at other times it seems like only a figment of his imagination, a hallucination.

His despair has become nausea, his nausea despair.

Siful has lost all hope. His strength is failing him. He could pass out at any moment, as several others on the boat already have. He does not know if he will be able to survive another night of these waves, this cold. The aeroplane has gone, there is only sky, sea, night and these waves, his stomach-ache and fear. The deep darkness of another night in the middle of the sea. He thinks of the phone calls he would like to make to his family when he arrives. He imagines his mother's voice on the other end of the line. She will be despairing, too, not having heard from him.

An inflatable boat carrying migrants from sub-Saharan Africa towards Europe.

THE PASSENGER   Annalisa Camilli

NO SAFE HAVEN

When the so-called Libyan coastguard service intercepts a vessel transporting migrants, what follows might not look like how you'd imagine a rescue operation to be conducted. Often the patrols shoot at the boats, and the migrants are beaten with sticks as they are brought aboard. The pushback operation that serves the European Union so well involves relocation to the infamous Libyan detention centres or to prisons. First-hand accounts, stories written by journalists and a UN investigative commission speak of human rights violations in these places. People suffer humiliation, torture, rape and execution in a context of entirely arbitrary treatment, partly as a consequence of the Libyan Civil War and political instability. These jails are either official or secret to varying degrees and have become a big business run by militias of former rebels, often in collaboration with people traffickers of the same nationalities as the fleeing migrants. In Libya anyone without a visa can be detained for an unspecified period without access to a lawyer. The inmates can be subjected to forced labour by the prison guards, who sell them to local businessmen, and migrants are held hostage by a system of criminal extortion. To free them and transport them to Europe the traffickers ask for thousands of dollars. The prisoners are lent mobile phones to contact relatives at home to ask for the sum being demanded on pain of death. But sometimes even paying is not enough because, rather than finding themselves on a boat heading for Europe, the unlucky ones are sent to another prison where the whole cycle begins again.

Whatever will they tell her? Whatever will she think? he wonders.

He learned to swim in the tanks that would fill up with rainwater during the rainy season, as all kids did where he's from, but he had never been in the sea before. He had no idea of the danger he was getting into. Now he doesn't know if he can bear another night in this hell. He touches the white beads around his neck. He is exhausted. He falls into a deep sleep.

In the middle of the night he is awoken by his comrades shouting. A ship is getting closer – he can see the lights; it is making the already rough sea even choppier. Someone takes the phone and through his tears calls for help.

The sun is rising again. The call drops. They try again, but the phone's battery is dying. They have been at sea for three days and three nights. Even the phone has forsaken them. They are doomed. The other ship knows that they're there, they've seen them, but no one knows if they will come and get them.

He thinks back to those hot days in Libya. The journey there had been smooth, taking a commercial flight from Qatar. At the airport he dialled the number of the Bangladeshi man who was supposed to come and get him. After waiting for over two hours he got into a pick-up truck and was driven to a two-roomed apartment that held around forty people, all of them Bangladeshi nationals waiting to set sail. The apartment was managed in shifts by a group of five armed Libyans. On the first night a guy with a gaunt face and a scar over his eyebrow had shoved the muzzle of a gun against him and demanded he hand over all his money. He had been warned of the risk of being robbed in Libya

ADRIFT

Not all migrants who cross the Mediterranean do so on old fishing vessels, inflatable boats or tramp freighters; in recent years the numbers of crossings by sailing boat have increased on the Turkish route. This mode of crossing is less conspicuous, safer, more comfortable and therefore more expensive. In the summer season sailing boats carrying dozens of Syrians, Afghans or Iraqis hidden in their holds mingle with the hundreds of tourist boats travelling between the Aegean and the Ionian, and a week after leaving they reach Italy, landing on the coast of Calabria or, more rarely, Salento. The skippers are very often Ukrainian, sometimes drawn in under false pretences and forced to become people traffickers on stolen boats in the Mediterranean. The Italian coastline is littered with boats of all sorts abandoned after landing and being seized by the authorities. At the mercy of bad weather, they soon become wrecks that threaten to pollute the environment, a fate that obviously applies to any boat carcass and not just those linked to migration. In 2018, for example, a powerful storm transformed the Ligurian port of Rapallo into a cemetery for boats destroyed by the waves. In order to dispose of them quickly the director of the port and others – who later became the subject of an investigation – engaged the services of individuals close to the Casalesi clan, a group within the Camorra, who broke down a number of wrecks without any concern for the impact of the resulting pollution and then used false documentation to transport the specialist waste to illegal dumps.

and had sewn some notes into a secret pocket in his clothes, but he paid the Libyan some money so he'd leave him alone.

The ship is getting closer. It is green, with three white stripes on the prow, a white bridge and a yellow mechanical arm. The waves rise higher, swelled by the wake of the ship.

Siful watches the boat draw nearer. The others get to their feet. There is a sudden euphoria. 'Help!' they shout, waving their arms.

The boy who had fainted has come to. Siful starts to stand up but immediately feels his legs give way beneath him. The boat lurches then capsizes. Plunge, splash.

He is underwater, salt gets in his mouth, cold runs up his spine. He kicks his legs and sinks even further. He can feel arms pushing him. He swims free, comes back up to the surface. The boat has capsized. The others, some of them already dead, are in the water.

He swims as he learned as a boy, moving his arms and legs non-stop to tread water, clinging to the grey wooden boat. He screams.

The green ship has sent out life-boats; they're coming to get them. An arm reaches out and pulls him into the inflatable. He is exhausted. When they get him on to the deck of the ship they notice he is struggling to walk and place him on a stretcher. His leg must be broken. Maybe a helicopter from Malta will come to take him to hospital, they say. But there is no helicopter.

There are many missing. He cannot see the boy who was in front of him on the boat. There are only seventeen of them. At least thirty aren't accounted for.

His leg is extremely painful. It slammed against the boat when he fell into the water. It is swollen. It might be broken, they say again. They help him take off his wet clothes, dry him, give him a blanket.

He is saved – but what about the others?

THE LIBYAN SAR

In Brussels the following day, during an EU Commission press briefing on the issue of migration, Italian journalist Eleonora Vasques asked the Commission's spokespersons why the emergency vessels of the European Union naval force operation, EUNAVFOR MED IRINI, did not go to rescue the boat, which sank thirty hours after Alarm Phone first alerted the authorities.

Since 2015 the EU naval force has been operating in international waters off the coast of Libya. Initially its primary mission was to disrupt human-trafficking networks by destroying the boats used by migrants. Often, however, European military vessels ended up going to the rescue of people in distress in that stretch of sea. In 2020 the operation was given a new name, IRINI, having previously been known as Sophia. Now the naval force's mission is to enforce the UN embargo on Tripoli and to disrupt the trade in arms and petroleum products, so European military vessels no longer go to the assistance of boats in distress, despite being obliged to do so under maritime law if they are the closest vessel to the incident. The force had been accused of acting as a 'pull factor', as if the migrants embarking from Libyan ports were doing so because of the presence of these ships and the prospect of being saved. The accusation has been disproved by several academic studies that show there is no correlation

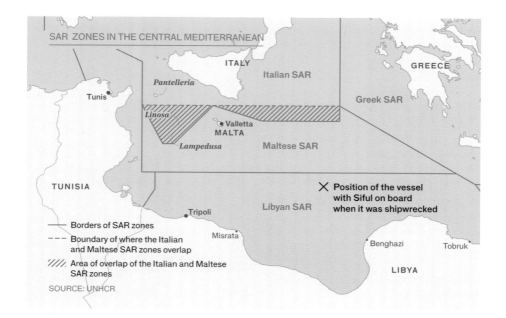

SAR ZONES IN THE CENTRAL MEDITERRANEAN

ITALY
Pantelleria
Tunis
Linosa
Valletta
MALTA
Lampedusa
Maltese SAR
Italian SAR
GREECE
Greek SAR

TUNISIA
Tripoli
Misrata
Libyan SAR

✕ Position of the vessel
with Siful on board
when it was shipwrecked

Benghazi   Tobruk
LIBYA

── Borders of SAR zones
--- Boundary of where the Italian
and Maltese SAR zones overlap
/// Area of overlap of the Italian and Maltese
SAR zones

SOURCE: UNHCR

between the presence of rescue ships and migration across the Mediterranean, but it continues to be weaponised by opponents of sea rescue. It is in part to steer clear of these accusations that EU ships fall short of their obligations and no longer undertake SAR operations in this area.

Peter Stano, spokesperson for the European Commission, replied to the Italian journalist, explaining that EU military ships cannot operate in Libyan territorial waters. In so doing he proved himself unaware of the fact that the limit of Libyan territorial waters is twelve nautical miles from the coast, and that the shipwreck on 11 March took place within Libya's so-called search-and-rescue zone, a vast area over which Libya does not exercise any sovereignty but has limited powers relating to SAR operations.

These are international waters in which rescue operations are supposed to be coordinated by the Libyan forces, despite the fact they lack the capability to do so for at least three reasons: (1) the Tripoli coastguard has no effective rescue coordination centre; (2) the Libyan coastguard does not exist as a single entity but is instead made up of multiple different coastguards, which often answer to or have relations with local militias; and (3) Libya cannot be considered a safe harbour in which shipwrecked people can disembark, as the country neither respects fundamental human rights nor is it party to the 1951 Refugee Convention. The Libyan SAR zone, in fact, was not recognised until May 2018, as the Tripoli government was not considered capable of coordinating rescue operations in such a vast stretch of sea. Since 2017, however, Italy and the EU have provided funding, training and rescue vessels to the Libyan coastguard with the express aim of delegating responsibility for SAR operations. According to a report from the NGO ActionAid, between 2017 and 2022 Italy paid Tripoli at least €124 million through various projects and missions.

Since 2017, as part of the two-phase, seven-year European programme Support to Integrated Border Management in Libya, Rome has spent €32.5 million of the €37 million received from Brussels on supplying Tripoli with rescue vessels. According to ActionAid and IrpiMedia, by the end of the seven years the total cost of the programme should amount to €67 million. The primary objective of the programme has been to build a rescue coordination centre in Tripoli and to equip the Libyan forces with patrol boats. It is clear that this has not been achieved, as the shipwreck of 11 March 2023 clearly demonstrates.

Libya still does not have a maritime rescue operations centre (MRCC) and is not capable of coordinating rescue missions along its 1,780 kilometres of coastline. It has no control, for instance, over Benghazi and the coasts of Cyrenaica. Despite the funds already spent, a document published in January 2023 by the European Commission itself acknowledges that the construction of the coordination centre in Tripoli has not been completed and that there are 'technical parts of an MRCC which have been delivered and are not used'.

Meanwhile, on 20 March 2023 – a few days after the boat sank northwest of Benghazi – Operation IRINI was renewed until 2025. Its budget was increased to more than €16 million, double that of Operation Sophia in 2016–17 but with half the number of military vessels.

'The European Union is ready to train the Libyan coastguard,' said Stano during the press conference of 20 March. 'Until now, the training of the Libyan coastguard was not taken up because of reasons on the Libyan side,' he explained.

'The implementation in this activity has not started due to the political fragmentation in Libya,' another source close to the European Commission confirmed to the news website Euractiv.

EUROPEAN COMPLICITY

28 April 2017. It is a sunny day in Gaeta.

Sandwiched between the sea and the walled city, on the terrace of the Bausan naval college barracks, Guardia di Finanza battalions stand in ranks facing the sea. The two patrol boats that Italy has donated to the Libyan coastguard are performing a carousel around the gulf with their sirens blaring.

A helicopter keeps close watch over the parade. The Italian minister of the interior, Marco Minniti, has travelled from Rome to attend the ceremony for the return of the two patrol boats, the first of many, to the Libyan coastguard. Italy first donated the boats in 2009, but, after being damaged in 2011 during the Libyan Civil War, they were returned to the Italians in 2012. Minniti gives a speech describing the Libyan coastguard as 'the most important structure in North Africa' for the management of irregular immigration. A little later the minister presents certificates to twenty Libyan cadets who, for the past three weeks, have been undertaking training in Gaeta.

The Italian government's intention, as declared in a Memorandum of Understanding with Libya signed in Rome on 2 February earlier that year, was to entrust the Libyan authorities with patrolling the coasts and intercepting the migrants that set sail every day on makeshift boats from North Africa towards Europe. Human rights groups

have described this practice as 'pushback by proxy'. In 2012, in fact, in the case of *Hirsi Jamaa and Others* vs. *Italy*, the European Court of Human Rights ruled that Italy had violated human rights principles by returning asylum seekers to Libya, where they suffered torture and inhumane and degrading treatment.

Entrusting Libya with the interception and rescue of migrant boats allows European authorities to sidestep this sort of verdict and to reduce the number of people arriving through the central Mediterranean, which was, in 2016, the primary route of irregular migration to Europe and the most dangerous in the world. Assigning responsibility for rescue operations in this area to the Libyan coastguard provides an excuse for EU rescue ships to retreat or fail to respond, as happened on 11 March 2023. It is no secret, however, that Italy and the EU support and coordinate the Libyan coastguard.

Over the past six years Rome has supplied Tripoli with twenty-four rescue vessels, and a further sixteen are forthcoming. At the beginning of February 2023 the Italian minister for foreign affairs, Antonio Tajani, his Libyan counterpart, Najla El Mangoush, and European Commissioner Olivér Várhelyi all attended a press conference at the Cantiere Navale Vittoria shipyard in Adria in northern Italy for the handover of one of these vessels, a Class 300 rescue boat, twenty metres long and six metres wide, capable of reaching a maximum speed of thirty-five knots bearing a full load of two hundred people.

THE EU ARMY

For much of its history the EU has not had any armed forces: after all, even symbolically, few things represent national sovereignty as effectively as a soldier in uniform. But in 2021 the European Border and Coast Guard Agency (Frontex to its friends – and enemies – from the French *Frontières extérieures*) was able to unveil brand-new uniforms featuring the EU stars on their blue background. This was because it has earned the gratitude of national governments by taking on part of a dirty job: pushing back migrants in contravention of the principle of non-refoulement enshrined in international law, which prohibits sending asylum seekers back to an unsafe country. Investigations by a number of journalists have shown that Frontex has been (and still is) complicit in illegal pushbacks of migrants who have already reached EU waters. In 2021 a report produced by the EU's anti-fraud office confirmed the systematic violation of migrants' human rights, leading to the resignation of its director, Fabrice Leggeri. But in spite of the criticism and a growing collection of scandals the EU states seem happy to use Frontex as a lightning rod, and the agency is expanding fast: in the seven-year period between 2022 and 2029 it will receive €5.6 billion compared with €100 million in 2014; the number of troops will grow from a thousand in 2014 to ten thousand – recruited directly by the agency – by 2027. If Frontex is destined to become the EU's first army, we can only hope that a minimum requirement would be for someone to instil in its culture a respect for human rights.

'European authorities have expanded a network of aerial surveillance across the central Mediterranean, but they have progressively withdrawn their rescue ships from the area, handing over responsibility to Libyan forces and obstructing the work of non-governmental rescue groups.'

But cooperation with the Libyan authorities goes beyond material support. According to several accounts, information exchanged between the European Border and Coast Guard Agency (Frontex), Operation IRINI and Libya has often allowed Libya to locate and force back migrant boats. In 2021, 32,400 people were intercepted at sea and forced back by Libyan forces, in part thanks to intelligence gathered by European authorities. Between 2013 and 2022, meanwhile, 26,000 people died or went missing at sea.

FRONTEX SURVEILLANCE
'About half an hour after we left we heard a drone over our head. It made a clear sound, Wzzzz Wzzzz. We were all afraid. Around noon we saw the drone. It stayed there about five minutes, did a circle or two. Two hours later a boat appeared: it was the Libyans,' says Abu Laila (not his real name), a twenty-eight-year-old Syrian who left Libya with another eighty migrants on a motorboat.

Abu Laila was rescued by Libyan patrol boats and taken back to Libya on 30 July 2021. At the time three NGO ships were operating in that stretch of sea: *Sea-Watch 3*, *Ocean Viking* and *Nadir*. According to the report *Airborne Complicity*, published by Human Rights Watch and Border Forensics, on that day there were at least five aeroplanes and a drone patrolling the sky. The drone had been flying over the western part of the Libyan SAR area since the early morning, following its regular route, while another was patrolling to the east of Malta and Misrata. The *Seabird 2* was also in the area, just as it was on 11 March 2023. The report states that the Frontex drone was the first of these to take off from its base in Malta. It is a large, grey craft, remotely operated from a ground-control station within the military section of the international airport on the island. The drone transmits almost-live footage and other information captured through optical and thermal sensors. All information is then sent to the Frontex headquarters in Warsaw where the data is analysed and decisions are made.

On the morning of 30 July 2021 the drone started heading south towards Libya at 2.52 a.m. (UTC+2). According to Human Rights Watch and Border Forensics this type of drone has been active since 2021. At 8 a.m. the drone deviated from its usual course, veering suddenly towards the northeast. It had probably noticed the small wooden boat for the first time. An hour later it was patrolling further to the north and did not return to the airport until 7.30 p.m.

No alert call was put out to the humanitarian and merchant ships in the area. Instead, according to Sea-Watch and others, at 1.28 p.m. Libyan coastguard patrol boat 648, the *Ras Jadir*, one of the four patrol boats that Italy had returned to Libya in 2017 after refurbishing them, arrived on the scene. The *Ras Jadir* intercepted a boat with twenty people on board. In footage shot from the *Seabird 2*, the *Ras Jadir* can be seen chasing the small wooden craft then launching an inflatable. No one was given a lifejacket, and all the migrants were taken on board.

An official European Union document, obtained by Human Rights Watch and Border Forensics, indicates that the *Ras Jadir* returned to the naval base in Tripoli at half past midnight with eighty-five people, having intercepted four boats carrying migrants. But none of the non-governmental rescue boats operating in the area that day received any alerts from Frontex or coastal authorities. The report says: 'The tracks of oil tankers *Superba* and *Inviken* and the supply ship *Belize* show they were in the vicinity, but none appears to have changed course, indicating they had not received any instructions to respond to a distress situation,' which they should have done under the law of the sea. Frontex did not send out any mayday alerts that day nor did it communicate with non-governmental rescue ships. The report continues: 'Between January 2020 and April 2022, Frontex says it issued twenty-one mayday alerts in the central Mediterranean, a tiny fraction of the boats sighted by its aerial surveillance. In 2021 alone, Frontex says there were 433 detections by aerial surveillance in the central Mediterranean involving 22,696 people.'

European authorities have expanded a network of aerial surveillance across the central Mediterranean, but they have progressively withdrawn their rescue ships from the area, handing over responsibility to Libyan forces and obstructing the work of non-governmental rescue groups. Operation IRINI ships are only active to the west of Libya, and now that people are once again departing from the ports of Tobruk and Derna, European ships do not undertake rescue missions, despite knowing that the Libyan coastguard does not operate in that stretch of sea. 'Faced with Frontex's fundamental opacity, we have analysed a vast set of flight tracking and other data to reconstruct its [surveillance] activities in the sky,' explained Giovanna Reder, a researcher at Border Forensics, at a press conference. 'Our analysis suggests that the Frontex drone played a key role in returning hundreds of people to Libya, condemning them to abuse and violence. The border agency and EU member states should be held accountable for this,' she concluded. 🖋

Liberté Toujours

From its heyday in the mid-20th century, over time Tangier lost its allure as the *enfant terrible* of the Mediterranean. But, after decades languishing in obscurity, it has in recent years reclaimed its international reputation, as the city, together with its port, strives to become an economic powerhouse, rediscovering the potential of its strategic location between two seas.

CHRISTIAN SCHÜLE
Translated by Stephen Smithson
Photography by Daniel Rodrigues

The view from the restaurant terrace of the Hotel Nord-Pinus in Tangier. All the photographs accompanying this article come from a feature published originally in *The New York Times*.

A hundred years ago Tangier was one of the most extraordinary cities in the world. The White City at the north-western tip of Africa was sung about, written about, talked about. Many came, some stayed, some came again, the famous and the not-so-famous: the writers, musicians, artists and fashion designers; the adventurers, entrepreneurs, heirs; gold dealers, transsexuals, hippies, spies, pederasts, pimps, fortune-hunters, philosophers, freaks, cranks, casual labourers and losers. In the medina, the old town, there were hundreds of banks and currency exchanges; there were equal numbers of Muslims, Jews and Christians, and there were almost as many synagogues and churches as mosques. They lived and they let live, and they accepted one another. Tangier became the place of longing on the Mediterranean.

Fifty years ago Tangier was a fallen, deflated and shunned place. Depression, dereliction, filth – the dark side of former joys. The world had turned to New York, Paris and London, while everything in the Kingdom of Morocco revolved around Casablanca and Rabat. Over Tangier lay the shadow of degradation and neglect.

Twenty years ago the shadow lifted, and the city began to bloom under artificial lighting. Millions and millions of dollars flowed into Tangier; boulevards and a new promenade were built. The world came back: European, American, Japanese and Chinese companies set up office there. The Saudi royal family invested and built residences; Arab princes came to the beach area. One of the largest ports on the African continent was created. Thousands of cars, aircraft components and wind turbines are now produced there daily. Tangier has been chosen and has woken up again.

In five years Tangier will be Africa's leading city, when construction of the new tech city – a platform for the automotive industry, aeronautics, e-commerce and global logistics – will be completed on 4,000 hectares of the city's northwestern edge. Further free-trade zones are to follow, and the technopark in the city centre will increase the number of green and e-technology startups it accommodates from fifty at present to perhaps as many as a hundred, while capacity at the two Mediterranean ports Tanger-Med I and II, at more than nine million containers, will be the largest in the entire Mediterranean region. Through its numerous free-trade zones, Morocco has in a short time developed from a traditional agricultural economy into a diversified industrial hub. While the former king, Hassan II, was still building dams and running an economy based on the expansion of traditional agriculture, his son, King Mohammed VI, has, since ascending the throne in 1999, focused on offshoring, outsourcing and global logistics. If all the indications are right, Tangier, with its uniquely privileged location on two major bodies of water, could, in the medium term, become one

CHRISTIAN SCHÜLE is a philosopher, writer and publicist. He worked at the German weekly *Die Zeit* before turning freelance, and his work has been published in such journals as *National Geographic*, *Mare* and *Geo*. He has written numerous books on topical issues much discussed in Germany, and his latest work, *Vom Glück, unterwegs zu sein* (Siedler, 2022), is a discussion on how and why humans love and need to travel.

DANIEL RODRIGUES is a Portuguese freelance photographer whose work takes him all over the world. Among the accolades he has been awarded are: first prize in the 'Daily Life' category of the World Press Photo award, 2013; third in the Photographer of the Year, Pictures of the Year International, 2015; and in 2017 he was the Ibero-American photographer of the year for POY LATAM. His work has been published in *The New York Times*, *The Wall Street Journal*, *The Washington Post* and by Al Jazeera.

of the geostrategic centres of a world currently being reordered.

How has all this been possible?

*

Some cities are overpowering, some over-demanding. Some stress, some impress, some bore. Some are vain, pretentious, obsessed with their own importance. Some are as endearing as they are seductive in their melancholy and nostalgia.

None of these things can be said of Tangier.

The city does not offer overwhelming architecture and beautiful ruins, and it does not make a show of itself with palazzo treasures, supersized galleries or architectural icons. Tangier has neither special allure nor exquisite charm; the almost immediate proximity of the Oriental and Occidental worlds means that both are only a proverbial stone's throw away: at the water's narrowest point Africa and Europe lie no more than thirteen kilometres apart. As the Maghreb's northern tip, Tangier is the crossing point from Orient to Occident and vice versa; the expanse that opens out, moving from the west and the south, into the arena for the great European myths – the *Mare Nostrum*. Lying on the shores of the Mediterranean, the White City has always offered the promise of sun and illumination, of trade with the West and with Africa.

*

Tangier wants nothing, demands nothing, offers no counsel, but some mysterious spirit that eludes definition immediately surrounds the visitor. In the squares, alleyways and streets an extraordinary ordinariness prevails, and the city has a strangely uninterested, almost blithe way of taking people captive. Why? Because it is Tangier. Tangier, you will often hear it said, speaks for itself. Tangier is Tangier. Tangier is unique, they say. And at some point it becomes clear: the essence of this city must be freedom – *liberté* and laissez-faire, from International Zone to free-trade zone, from top to bottom – even if state spies sit in the cafés reporting on anything suspicious and foiling revolutions.

*

The cigarette vendor starts his day's work early in the morning. Seen by all, disturbed by nobody, roughly every five minutes he passes the Gran Café de Paris, the hinge joining Tangier's old and new towns, to the Place de France. A short man of around fifty, moustachioed and with O-shaped legs, serious-looking, wearing a shirt and red jacket, he does nothing more than come and go, glancing now and again out of the corner of his eye. In his hands he holds two blue cartons of Gauloises Blondes. Nothing – and nobody – escapes him. At the tables of the Gran Café itself, which faces the French embassy and has been a meeting

> 'That ten-minute walk takes you from traditional Tangier to globalised Tangier, and without any warning you stumble into a strange and unfamiliar world.'

place for businessmen, intellectuals and artists since 1927, local men and tourists of both sexes sit in front of their glasses of mint tea at all times of day and watch the bottleneck at the roundabout: police-men with whistles, mint-coloured Dacia taxis, SUVs with dark-tinted windows, anarchic scooters and the odd donkey cart. Mobile traders with wheelbarrows pass by, offering packs of Tempo hand-kerchiefs, raincoats, melons and almond cakes; then *mesdames* in leather boots and Ray-Bans, followed by Black African women in veils and teenagers in loosely draped headscarves. Again and again you see tradition-conscious Berbers in djellabas with pointed hoods crossing the street from the café, and at some point a *monsieur* in patent-leather shoes is sure to come and place his hat on the table.

Sometimes the cigarette vendor goes without his red jacket, sometimes he leans on a post, and at some point you cease to notice him. He trades his wares quietly and discreetly but successfully. If he sells each single cigarette for two dirham (*c.* 20 US cents) and a pack costs him thirty-five dirham, then each pack of twenty Gauloises earns him five dir-ham profit, or just about 50 cents. Work-ing ten hours a day and selling one pack every hour, he can expect to earn roughly $5 a day or $35 a week – not a bad income if you consider that the average monthly wage in Morocco is around $330, espe-cially since gross and net are probably the same for a cigarette vendor.

Whenever he disappears for a few

minutes into Rue de la Liberté, the same group of homeless people enter the scene, as though they are the next act on the bill, and they walk past the café to the one public waste bin, where they rummage for cans and bottles to knock back whatever liquid remains. One of them, a really feral-looking man draped in blankets, studies the waiters' posi-tions before grabbing a half-emptied glass of water from a table that has just become free, emptying it in one gulp and hastily putting it back. The other-wise extremely vigilant waiters appear unconcerned, deliberately wait for a few seconds, then clear up and wipe the table surface for the next guest to come and leave the next glass of water for the next homeless person to grab.

*

To the right of Place de France, Rue de la Liberté leads towards the old town. From the Liberté, going right again, Rue Salah Eddine Al Ayoubi takes the incline down to the bottom, where it meets the four-lane Avenue Mohammed VI run-ning parallel to the Mediterranean coast. That ten-minute walk takes you from traditional Tangier to globalised Tan-gier, and without any warning you stum-ble into a strange and unfamiliar world.

Avenue Mohammed VI is the sym-bol of a newly reawakened, polished city that looks like it is breaking out and heading straight into the future. Along the avenue posters on barrier walls advertise the planned Tanja Marina Bay as a new luxury residential area. There

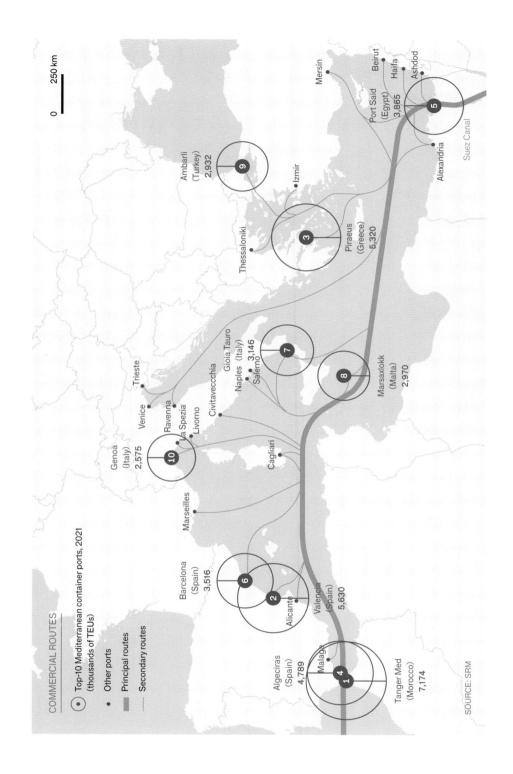

COMMERCIAL ROUTES

⊙ Top-10 Mediterranean container ports, 2021
  (thousands of TEUs)

• Other ports

▬ Principal routes

— Secondary routes

0   250 km

Mersin

Beirut
Halfa
Ashdod

Port Said
(Egypt)
3,865

5

Suez Canal

Alexandria

Ambarli
(Turkey)
2,932

9

Izmir

Thessaloniki

3

Piraeus
(Greece)
5,320

Trieste

Venice

Ravenna

La Spezia

Genoa
(Italy)
2,575

10

Livorno

Civitavecchia

Gioia Tauro
(Italy)

Naples

Salerno
3,146

7

Marsaxlokk
(Malta)
2,970

8

Cagliari

Marseilles

Barcelona
(Spain)
3,516

6

2

Alicante

Valencia
(Spain)
5,630

Algeciras
(Spain)
4,789

Malaga

1 **4**

Tanger Med
(Morocco)
7,174

SOURCE: SRM

Liberté Toujours

THE PASSENGER   Christian Schüle

Opposite: The bar at Number One, a restaurant close to the seafront in Tangier.
Above: A carpet seller in Rue Sebou.

are no buildings yet, but there are computer simulations – and powerful excavators clearing away soil overgrown with wildflowers and weeds.

The idea of the new Tangier was first floated long ago. The urban development vision of this waterfront scheme comes from the Abu Dhabi-based Eagle Hills group – a business active in Jordan, Ethiopia, Bahrain and the United Arab Emirates that specialises in seafront developments for a globalised clientele – with a façade design that it calls Facelift. In keeping with the spirit of urban cosmetic surgery, the distinguished Royal Yacht Club de Tanger – founded in 1925 as the first yacht club on the African continent – has been reconceived on a site that was previously neglected and overgrown, with a jetty reaching out into the sea, complete with covered car-park facilities, providing top-class culinary and DJ entertainment for the new-rich and medium-rich upper class of international tourism. Smaller yachts are moored in the marina, and nothing obstructs the view of cruise ships at anchor. For this development, which has no Oriental character at all and has been criticised by Tangierians as sterile, the neighbouring fishing harbour was torn down and with it much of the local identity. The old wooden boats bore the names of Tangier seamen, and the old stalls – their squid and prawn dishes the stuff of legend – were social hubs.

Having been moved a few hundred metres east, the fishing port was recently reopened. Against the white of its concrete-block construction, which might almost have been inspired by Bauhaus aesthetics, the colourfully painted fishing boats and trawlers seem like antiquated foreign bodies.

When global lifestyle is advanced at the expense of tradition, the result can be described, according to one's viewpoint, as either cultural vandalism or farsightedness. Whichever way one chooses to see it, Tangier's systematic transformation for a new era is the vision of one man.

*

The Moroccan king is, naturally, above criticism, and it is rare to hear anyone expressing an opinion about him or his ideas that is anything other than positive. Born in 1963, Mohammed VI (M6, as people like to call him), who lends his name to the coastal avenue, is seen as father figure, popular hero and the nation's saviour. The first anecdote that most people relate about him dates from when he was as new to the throne as he was young. During a car journey along the old promenade of the still rundown, shady Tangier, he is said to have remarked that he couldn't see his sea for all the buildings. The date of this episode varies according to who is telling it, but it must have taken place between 2000 and 2002. To cut the rest of the story short, the skyscrapers in the first row – with their hotels, kiosks, discos, clubs, bars and restaurants – were reduced by half shortly afterwards. Then, because the result still did not allow full and panoramic views of the Mediterranean, all the buildings were razed as part of a modernisation programme to bring the area into line with the zeitgeist. Some of the establishments affected went underground, as it were, but the Bling Bling Luxury Club and Golden Beach Club remain to this day.

The new beach promenade looks, unsurprisingly, like something from a globalised architectural practice, a computer-generated visualisation

The Mediterranean lost its central position in global trade to ocean routes and larger markets centuries ago, but the traces of its long-standing mercantile tradition have not disappeared. Two of the world's three largest maritime transport companies are Mediterranean: the French firm CMA CGM, based in Marseilles, and the Mediterranean Shipping Company, or MSC, founded by the Neapolitan businessman Gianluigi Aponte but headquartered in Switzerland. And so a landlocked country controls the world's largest shipping company by total capacity. Established in 1970 with just one ship trading between Naples and Somalia, in 2022 MSC overtook the Danish firm Maersk, which has over a century of history behind it. And its lead is set to increase, as the two companies have decided not to renew their alliance, which dates back to 2015, and have adopted very different strategies: while Maersk will concentrate its investments on services in ports and along the rail and road networks, MSC is aiming to increase the total capacity of its fleet to gain further market share and cut costs with greater economies of scale. The Mediterranean-Swiss company also has a cruise line, MSC Cruises, and owns shares in various transport companies that ferry goods and passengers around the Mediterranean, such as the Italian firms Moby Lines (which it saved from bankruptcy in 2022), SNAV, Grandi Navi Veloci and Caremar, which operates the ferries in the Gulf of Naples. So if you are on holiday in the Med, be sure to go via Switzerland.

made real, the palms now replaced by thin-stemmed, tentacle-like lamp-posts standing at regular intervals. In the buildings on the other side of an avenue constantly busy with traffic, the vacancy rate is high: lifeless shops and takeaway kiosks that attract few visitors are a sad reality. Along with the palm trees thousands of prostitutes disappeared, and with them frivolity and lightness – so run the complaints of old Tangierians – and the sensual exuberance of an extravagant and popular nightlife.

M6, having decided to break with the policies of his father Hassan II following the latter's death in 1999, shifted the focus away from Casablanca and Rabat back towards the north, putting Tangier, by that time half forgotten, at the centre of his country's economic and social resurgence in a bid to become Africa's leading economic nation following Libya's collapse. With money from the Saudi royal family, the UAE and China, the state set about building roads, playgrounds, bridges and a new station for Africa's first high-speed TGV line, from Tangier to Rabat. In the past ten years air-conditioned malls have been added, while newly built interlocked apartment complexes six-to-ten storeys high now line up outside the city. Since M6 took charge of royal business affairs and started developing Tangier as Africa's gateway to the world and the world's portal into Africa, the once small town stretching over seven hills has grown (rather too prolifically, some say) into a metropolis with around a million inhabitants. Twenty years ago, the story runs, there was no paving in the city. Today, however, there are swept pavements everywhere, and on the promenade, which is hardly ever used for promenading, a beautiful bench is placed with almost Germanic precision every thirty metres. When the air is clear you can see the sun reflected in the windows of the houses of the Andalusian villages across the strait; when the light is good Europe is within reach. However, it is no longer the British and French who come to Tangier but the Arabs and Chinese. This is the current answer to the question – *Who comes to Tangier, when do they come and from where?* – from which it has always been possible to read the shifting relationships within the world's grammar, its values and on what it places importance.

*

Tangier is the city on two waters, and every inner illumination is known to begin with light. Under the sun's influence the Mediterranean mist blends with its saline Atlantic counterpart to create an otherworldliness that is at times magical. The light is so special that when, in 1912, the French painter Henri Matisse, having experienced a pro-found mental crisis, spent an extended winter in the Grand Hotel Villa de France on the edge of the medina, it inspired him to go in search of himself, sparking a kind of rebirth that led him to a new art in which he discovered a unique, overwhelming blue. The deliciously delicate, pastel-soft light of Tangier made Matisse a man freed from doubt.

For the melancholy painter, inner illumination and awakening took place just before the First World War, when around sixty thousand people lived in the city – twenty thousand Muslims, twenty thousand Christians, twenty thousand Jews. As far as is known there were no quarrels or conflict. In Tangier, people say, one readily begins a sentence in Arabic, carries it on in Spanish and then ends it in French (or any permutation thereof). The late Rachel Muyal, *grande dame* of Tangier and long one of the city's great intellectual figures, once recounted how, when she was young, a Muslim man whom she did not know came up to her and kissed her forehead, the forehead of a Jewish woman, just like that, in the middle of the street. Then he went on his way.

*

Respect, freedom to find oneself and the freedom that one finds for oneself, these are the things of which so many have spoken, and so many speak, who have come to Tangier and never left. Over the decades the paradox of Tangierian *liberté* has taken on a life of its own and assumed mythic status. This is how it goes. You come to Tangier to stay, even though you really intended to leave. Tangier is a place of transfer that does not let go. Tangier is a place of transit that locks you in tightly. In a figurative sense this is where cars are sold,

'Twenty years ago, the story goes, there was no paving in the city. Today, however, there are swept pavements everywhere, and on the promenade a beautiful bench is placed with almost Germanic precision every thirty metres.'

connecting flights are cancelled and life plans are jettisoned.

Paul Bowles, the American novelist and composer, is an example of someone who never in any way intended to live long-term in Tangier; it just happened. Bowles came in 1947 because both post-war USA and post-war Paris had ceased to interest him. In Tangier he wrote his celebrated novel *The Sheltering Sky,* lived with his wife Jane in different hotels and finally alone in an apartment block on the New Mountain, where, after fifty years in the city, he died in 1999. The Anglo-Canadian painter Brion Gysin visited Bowles in Tangier for a week in 1950 – and then stayed for a further twenty-three years. Twenty years ago the Parisian writer Simon-Pierre Hamelin spent a few days visiting a friend in Tangier; today he runs the legendary bookstore Librairie des Colonnes. In 1994 the Belgian Vincent Coppée arrived from Brussels in his Land Rover intending to travel onwards to Cape Town the next day. He stayed for a week, met the director of the American School and has now been running the El Morocco Club in the kasbah for twenty-five years. This one-time notorious drug sinkhole has now been gentrified but has, like all the buildings in the district, always been architecturally and metaphorically dominated by the citadel, which has ever been a symbol of both religious and political power.

And native Tangierians who had moved to Paris or New York have returned, and more are coming – like Farida Benlyazid, the renowned director of comedies and documentaries, an elegant, stylishly dressed woman in her seventies who, while pulling a thin cigarette from a case, describes the essence of her city in two words: curiosity and tolerance.

*

A sober glance in the annals reveals that Tangier attained near world-historical significance in 1923 when the city was declared an International Zone. As a special administration zone, it became from that point an enclave of legal and moral permissiveness within the authoritarian Kingdom of Morocco. In the Interzone, as the whole of Tangier was known, there was a control committee, a management board and a supreme administrator – a position occupied at different times by representatives of France, Spain, The Netherlands, Portugal and Belgium. There were French, Jewish and Arabic law courts but no income tax, customs duty or restrictions on currency exchange. Petit Socco, the square in the very heart of the medina, housed more than four hundred banks and four thousand trading firms, including the German and French postal services. Here newspaper boys ran around, boxing matches were held, betting on horse racing flourished, gold dealers did business in the streets and there were, as was widely known, numerous brothels providing boys to pederasts from Europe and the USA.

Opposite: Fruit and vegetable stalls in Tangier's medina.
Above: The celebrated Librairie des Colonnes in Boulevard Pasteur.

The two Spanish enclaves on the North African coast, Ceuta and Melilla, each with a population of around 85,000, have been Spanish territory since the 15th century. Over the past thirty years they have enjoyed a special derogation from the Schengen Treaty allowing residents in the Moroccan provinces of Tétouan and Nador to enter without a visa. But pressure on the border is not so much from the locals as from migrants, often from outside Morocco, who want to reach these little outposts of Europe on the African continent in order to claim asylum in the EU. By mutual agreement the border has become increasingly militarised since the 1990s, which is why suspicions were immediately raised when, in May 2021, more than eight thousand people entered Ceuta in the space of thirty-six hours. The theory was that it was an act of revenge on the part of King Mohammed VI, who was irritated that Spain had agreed to offer medical treatment to the leader of the liberation movement of Western Sahara, a contested territory. The border was mostly closed between 2020 and 2022 as a result of Covid-19, and Spain is now moving towards an abolition of the derogation from the Schengen Treaty, which is already making life more difficult for the Moroccans in neighbouring areas who work in or have links with Ceuta and Melilla. The two enclaves are almost four hundred kilometres apart and quite different: Ceuta is regarded as more problematic, with both the murder rate and the proportion of votes for the far-right Vox party higher than anywhere else in Spain, whereas Melilla enjoys more serene multicultural cohabitation.

Tangier, unimpressed by itself, beamed like a promise. Diplomatic missions of all kinds were in the Zone – radio stations, espionage operations, agents, negotiators, Nazis and communists. During the Spanish Civil War in the late 1930s, as people will still tell you to this day, Franco-supporting fascists would sit at the Café Central while socialist Republicans would sit at the Café Fuentes opposite, the two sides throwing bottles at one another. The Interzone was a demilitarised area under international control, a self-governing territory. Morocco was a protectorate of France, but Tangier was excluded from this arrangement. Tennessee Williams, in despair at the failure of Moroccan boys to fall in love with him, later wrote *Cat on a Hot Tin Roof* and *Suddenly Last Summer* somewhere in the Petit Socco – while William Burroughs, in Room 3 of the El Munira Hotel, when not railing about Arabs in his letters, was completing his masterpiece, *Naked Lunch*. At Café Hafa smugglers would roll packages of hashish down the hill of the medina into waiting boats, while all kinds of turmoil and crises in a Europe tearing itself apart brought the displaced, the persecuted and the exiled to Tangier with their traumas, stories and hopes – which is why, as it happens, it was the model for the location of *Casablanca*, although the famous film's producers chose another Moroccan city's name because it sounded more poetic.

In 1956 the city was incorporated into Morocco, which had now achieved independence from France. A few years later the banks closed and the Interzone was no more, leaving the enclave of laissez-faire to fade and fall into squalor and decay within a Morocco that was, until M6, a royal dictatorship with torture chambers and traditional agriculture.

*

As before, there are neglected neighbourhoods, run-down alleys, dilapidated houses with windows blanked out, and people from all regions of Morocco and Africa still come here to try their luck, because Tangier is considered the most liberal city in the most liberal Arab country. The smell of Tangier, people say, is as distinctive as its light is legendary – the air impregnated with the mist from two waters and the fresh fish wafting in from the central market hall. At Cape Spartel in the west, the ocean water of the Atlantic is more silvery; at Cape Malabata in the east, the seawater of the Mediterranean is a hearty blue. Between the two, in an extravagant sweep, stretches a crescent-shaped bay lined with a sandy beach where a delicate surf frolics.

It is here that Hercules, the heroic shaper of the world, is said to have used the power of his muscles to tear Europe and Africa apart, for reasons now lost to us. He lived, so the historian-poets of antiquity suggest, in the bottomless cave at Cape Sparta, where the beatniks held costume parties in the 1960s and – so legend has it – fear of scorpions led the phobia-prone Truman Capote to get Allen Ginsberg, Jack Kerouac and Paul Bowles to carry him down the slope like an emperor in a sedan chair knocked together from wooden slats.

Right now, by the Mediterranean at the eastern edge of the city, highly trained young male boxers, engaging in their evening workouts, compete for attention – although, as far as the women nearby are concerned, it is the horses trotting stoically on the beach that are most worthy of interest. A female tourist rides in a leisurely manner into the rising moon when the muezzins, competing with the clamour of seagulls and the chirping of sparrows and crickets, begin their call to prayer. A first voice starts up and soars an octave higher, while four more join in, and a swelling chant pours over the city: *Allah is most great; come to salvation*. It's more businesslike than missionary. In Tangier morality is good but trade is better. Of course, limitless freedom exists nowhere, but in Tangier everything seems possible because everything has always been possible. In 1777 Morocco, under the sultanship of Muhammad ben Abdallah, became the first nation to recognise the newly independent United States of America. A few years later the US opened a diplomatic mission, the new country's first international legation, in the medina. Tangier consequently became a port of call for American overseas freight, thus breaking Britain's Gibraltar monopoly.

*

Tangier's destiny is to exist as a zone of freedom. If what was unleashed a hundred years ago in this myth-protected space was a libertinage that attracted all free spirits, *liberté* as defined today comes via skilfully organised free trade in selected sectors. Tangier (the city as well as the wider Tangier-Tétouan region) at present has three separate free-trade zones. The largest of these lies in the west of the city, at the edge of the Atlantic, and comprises seven sections in which work is carried out around the clock by sixty thousand people working in three shifts daily. Strictly speaking, each of these zones now exists not as Moroccan territory but as an international inter-realm with its own set of rules, which is why the entrances and exits are monitored and the zones are fenced off with barbed wire. Anyone wishing to enter must register in advance and bring their passport.

A free-trade zone is a calculated win-win project. State and enterprise alike benefit from terms tailored to meet the needs of both: investments in return for subsidies, location in return for jobs. For the multinationals and smaller firms that settle in a free-trade zone the attractions are enormous. Motorway transport through Morocco between the zones and Tanger Automotive City (TAC) is free of customs duty and tax.

First incentive: lower labour costs. Compared with Europe wage costs and pay rates are low. In the Tangier Free Zone, for example, the minimum hourly rate for a machine operator is thirteen dirhams ($1.30). In France it would be many times higher.

Second incentive: low social-security contributions. If a business signs an employment contract with a Moroccan worker through the state employment agency, no employer's social security contributions are payable for that worker for two years. The contributions are paid from a state fund dedicated to supporting young Moroccans after graduation and securing them the first-class training that the mainly European companies can provide. Perhaps they will then go on one day to set up their own firms, create jobs and help keep the Moroccan economy going. In the third year of employment the businesses meet just half the costs of their trainees' sickness and unemployment insurance and pension contributions. In this way the state promotes the training and further development of highly qualified, skilled workers, of which there is a shortage in Europe.

Third incentive: full exemption from tax and customs duty. Businesses settling in a Tangier free-trade zone are exempt from tax for the first five years, after which tax is payable at the low rate of 8.75 per cent for the subsequent fifteen years – compare that with 36 per cent outside the zones. Businesses in the zone do not have to pay import taxes on raw materials, customs duties on imported machinery or VAT for the construction of their production and warehousing facilities. In return, every business based in a free-trade zone must commit to buying 60–80 per cent of its raw materials for production in Morocco – an arrangement from which the domestic market profits.

Fourth incentive: custom-fitted infrastructure. Tangier's three free-trade zones have specialised predominantly in infrastructure for the automotive industry and aeronautics. The Moroccan state ensures, through a constantly expanding network, ideal production conditions and a frictionless value-added chain. Outside the zones, components would have to be transported by road over hundreds or even thousands of kilometres. Within the zones, in contrast, producers of everything needed for automobile production are at hand – suppliers from Japan, Germany, Spain and France producing oil pumps, cables, seals, injection mouldings, bodywork, packaging, upholstery, automotive paint and plastics. This guarantees short distances, low transport costs, high production efficiency and increased productivity. The car industry can offer its products at lower prices in Europe, allowing increased unit sales to drive revenue growth. The first car maker to come to

'Businesses have left Europe and moved here, and there are no places left in the existing free-trade zones – but new zones are now being created.'

Tangier was Renault/Nissan, which in 2012 moved a large part of its production from France. In the TAC free-trade zone specially designed for the group it now produces 400,000 vehicles annually. One of the welcoming gifts from the state was a newly built railway for the new plant linking it with the port nearby.

Fifth incentive: geographical location. The distance from the free-trade zones to the Mediterranean using the newly built motorways is between twenty and twenty-five kilometres, and then Europe across the sea at its narrowest point is just thirteen kilometres away. Goods produced in the Tangier zones can be exported to the European market within a very short time. Tangier lies on the Atlantic at the point where it narrows before entering the Mediterranean, and its port lies directly on the sea, without a flow path. This enables deep-draft container ships to dock and unload their cargos without losing time on an access route. Because demand had outgrown the Tanger MED I port, the new MED II was built, fitted out with the most innovative terminal technology and opened in 2019. Tanger MED I/II is now the largest port in Africa. There is no longer any reason to use the Andalusian port and industrial city of Algeciras.

*

From the boardrooms of French or German companies in the free-trade zones over the past twenty years, it has become increasingly common to hear reports of huge increases in Tangier's level of industrialisation and improvements to its working standards, of how several businesses have left Europe and moved here and how there are no places left in the existing zones – but new zones are now being created. In fact, there is even going to be a new city built on a site a few kilometres north of Tangier along the motorway heading towards the port. The village of Ain Dalia currently stands on the site, but there are plans to move its inhabitants in three to four years, clear away the farms and shacks, and then Cité Mohammed VI Tanger Tech will be ready for its new occupants. A large part of the two thousand hectares of space is to go to two hundred Chinese enterprises in the sectors of aerospace, electromobility, electronics and solar energy; the talk is of 100,000 newly created jobs and $1 billion in annual investments. In total, 300,000 people will be able to live in what will be a 'smart city' divided into zones and sectors; it will be a residential as well as an industrial hub. For China, Cité Tanger Tech is another prize link in the chain, another major step forward for its policy of creating a New Silk Road and conquering Africa through economic cooperation. The new strategic partnership between Morocco and China was sealed by M6 and President Xi Jinping in Beijing in May 2016.

*

The streetlamps in the alleyways around the boulevard between Gran Café de Paris and the Mediterranean come on with a promptness that unsettles, their

Roofs of the kasbah in Tangier.

THE GREAT DISAPPOINTMENT

While the Moroccan monarchy has relaunched the country's economy under M6, growth in Tunisian GDP has been much flatter in recent decades. Tunisia had seemed to be the only example of a successful Arab Spring: in 2011 the Jasmine Revolution removed the dictator Zine al-Abidine Ben Ali, in 2014 a secular, pluralist constitution was approved and the year after that the Tunisian National Dialogue Quartet was awarded the Nobel Peace Prize. Then the economic crisis, the terrorist attacks of 2015, public spending cuts imposed by the IMF and ongoing accusations of corruption brought Kais Saied to power in 2019. Regarded as an anti-establishment outsider, since 2021 he has imposed a new authoritarian approach that is dismantling the young democracy, dissolving both parliament and the Supreme Judicial Council, approving a new constitution that centralises power and prevents impeachment and repressing dissent with waves of arrests. While the first free elections achieved brightness bursting through the twilight. The cigarette vendor continues to come and go. Meanwhile, just a few streets away, in front of the entrance to a living-room-sized bar with no name, which only insiders know about, the legendary hash dealer Sultan sits in a wheelchair. The old man chats with police; the secret agents of the state are always close by. Sultan goes about his business with the freedom of one who is unassailable, and he is left alone. Everybody knows everything, but nobody talks about it. Everything is allowed, provided it is not spoken of publicly. Women with their heads uncovered smoke in public and smoke hashish in the bars of the medina like the twenty-somethings once did. Pederasts from every country still wait in the cafés for pubescent Moroccan shoeshiners. To this day the souks spill over into the downhill-running sidestreets, some of them just two metres wide – Rue Kadi, Rue Mokhtar Aharden, Rue Touahin. The houses are plastered in ochre or whitewashed and painted blue, red or green at street level. On tiled walls flowerpots hang in cast-iron brackets; there is always a broom sweeping somewhere. The shops selling leather goods, trinkets and jewellery, lit with an overwhelming splendour, are often no bigger than a storage cupboard. And out of nowhere a guy rushes into the middle of the Rue Siaghine on the Petit Socco in the medina, as unbidden as he is gregarious.

'*Amigo*, hotel?'

Shake of the head.

'*Restaurant, amigo? Tagine? Couscous?*'

Resolute shaking of the head. He places his hand on my arm.

'*Non, merci*. No thanks.'

My most regrettable refusal elicits a smile.

'*Amigo, cocaine?*' he whispers.

A stern look from me.

No deal then but an elaborate handshake.

'Where are you from?' he asks in English.

'Germany.'

'Deutschland!'

'Is that something special?' I ask in return.

'Brother,' he says in German, 'I love Merkel. I love the SPD.'

Above the Strait of Gibraltar, over the Mediterranean, the sun floats out of view, and the freighters, trawlers and tankers drift away, while out on the crescent-shaped bay between Cape Spartel and Cape Malabata a few seagulls hail a returning fishing boat with mad laughter. Then evening comes in. But there will always be a new morning – that is the myth of Tangier. It is the myth of freedom. 🐦

a 74 per cent turnout, this collapsed to a miserable 11 per cent in 2023, a clear sign of the sense of disillusionment among the Tunisian population. In search of a scapegoat, Saied has blamed sub-Saharan migrants, even recycling the conspiracy-theory rhetoric of the 'great replacement' with his talk of a 'plot to change the demographic composition of Tunisia in an attempt to turn it into simply an African country and erase its Arab and Muslim nature', words that were followed by outbreaks of intimidation and racist violence throughout the country.

The Invention of the Mediterranean Diet

The Mediterranean diet, which features on UNESCO's Intangible Cultural Heritage list, is the world's best-known and most comprehensively studied dietary model – and possibly the most misunderstood. But what the creators of the myth actually realised, in spite of the scientific limitations of their research and their Eurocentric prejudices, is that what underpins Mediterranean gastronomic culture is communal eating.

RACHEL RODDY
Photography by Piero Percoco

Wheat, barley, spelt, peas, lentils, chickpeas, broad beans, olive oil, cardoons, chard, purslane, lettuce, endives, asparagus, carrots, garlic, onions, turnips, celery, cabbages, pomegranates, quinces, almonds, pistachios, dates, figs, grapes, vine leaves, honey, goats, beef, sheep, poultry, eggs, milk, cheese, butter, salt, game, deer, antelopes, gazelles, wild boar, grasses, roots, tubers, seeds, pears, apples, walnuts, hazelnuts, chestnuts, date palms, fish, shellfish and crustaceans, citrus fruits, rice, sugar, pasta, spinach, aubergines, cocoa, chocolate, sorghum, millet, couscous, carob, jujubes, limes, citrons, peaches, apricots, plums, cherries, azaroles, medlars, whitecurrants and blackcurrants, green beans, peas, cauliflowers, cucumbers, melons and water melons, cumin, caraway and aniseed, henna, saffron, oregano, myrtle, jasmine, roses, narcissi, water lilies, goldenrod, wallflowers, marjoram, violets, lilies, thyme, opium poppies and Indian hemp, pepper, cloves, ginger, nutmeg, cassia, manna, rhubarb, aloes, gum, maize, tomatoes, potatoes, peppers, prickly pears, beans, squash, myrtle, paprika, new types of olives, coffee, tea.

(A Mediterranean shopping trolley, inspired by the chapter 'History of Mediterranean Food' by Yassine Essid in *MediTERRA: The Mediterranean Diet for Sustainable Regional Development*, edited by the International Centre for Advanced Mediterranean Agronomic Studies and published by Presses de Sciences PO, 2012)

I t began 5.3 million years ago with subsidence and the most spectacular flood, which breached a mountain range and filled a basin. It also began in Rome in 1951, at a United Nations conference dedicated to the nutritional rehabilitation of Europe after the Second World War, when Ancel Keys from the University of Minnesota met Gino Bergami from the Institute of Medicine in Naples.

The two doctors met in Rome. Had they not, the words 'Mediterranean' and 'diet' might never have been placed next to each other – at least, not in the way we've come to understand them when placed together, whatever that may be! Decades later Keys, who chaired the conference, would recount his first exchange with Bergami in his memoir, *Adventures of a Medical Scientist: Sixty Years of Research in Thirteen Countries*. There are only a few copies in existence, one of which is in the hands of the anthropologist Elisabetta Moro, whose detailed work on Keys opens a window

RACHEL RODDY is a British journalist, food writer, photographer and cook who has lived in Rome and Sicily since 2005. She began food writing on her blog *Rachel Eats* and since 2015 has had a weekly column in the *Guardian* entitled 'Tales from an Italian Kitchen'. She has published three books on Italian food: *My Kitchen in Rome* (Grand Central Life & Style, 2016, USA), titled *Five Quarters* in the UK (Headline Home, 2015), which won the André Simon Memorial Fund Award, *Two Kitchens* (Headline, 2019, USA / Headline Home, 2017, UK) and *An A-Z of Pasta* (Knopf, 2023, USA / Fig Tree, 2021, UK).

PIERO PERCOCO is a self-taught photographer whose journey began in 2012 when he started posting on Instagram photographs of everyday life that he shot on an iPhone. Over the years this turned into a job, and he has since worked with numerous newspapers and journals such as *The New Yorker*, *The New York Times* and the *British Journal of Photography*. He has published several books, including *The Rainbow Is Underestimated* (Skinnerboox, 2019).

into his life, offering a slice of social history that can be interpreted in a number of ways: revolutionary, useful, problematic, something to be dismissed, all four.

In the memoir Keys recalls one of the conference sessions – which was primarily focused on food shortages and vitamin deficiencies – in which he brought up the relationship between heart disease and diet, revealing a shocking statistic: in the USA at the time heart attacks were the cause of death of 50 per cent of men aged between the ages of thirty-nine and fifty-nine. This fact 'aroused no particular interest' among the delegates with exception of Bergami, who noted that heart disease wasn't a problem in Naples, that hospital cases of heart attacks could be counted on the fingers of one hand. After the conference Keys, who was on sabbatical in the UK, wrote to Bergami, keen for more details. 'Come and check for yourself!' was Bergami's challenge, and so started a friendship and research partnership that would last a lifetime. Keys wrote back: 'We are coming!' True to his word, a few weeks later Keys and his wife, the biologist Margaret Haney, packed their newly acquired Hillman Minx and drove, stopping in Paris, Strasbourg, the Swiss Alps, Milan, Bologna, Florence and Rome before arriving in Naples. Original language fails many of us on arriving in Italy, and Keys describes the final leg of the journey in standard, emblematic style: 'Passing through snow-capped mountains on one side, the blue splendour of the sea on the other, separated in the middle by trees laden with oranges.'

The sea, which takes us back to the beginning. The tectonic fault that caused a flood which filled a basin creating a sea *in mezzo alle terre*, 'in the middle of the lands', the Mediterranean just one of its many names past and present. There is something foetal about the shape of the Mediterranean – at an early stage captured by ultrasound scan, with a strange, elongated head and one arm raised – although the comparison doesn't really evoke the meticulous details of bays, straits and the thousands of islands. Its shape is fundamental. Wide enough to support vastly different civilisations and yet narrow enough to allow close contact, these proportions are why the Mediterranean became, in historian David Abulafia's opinion in his work *The Great Sea*, probably 'the most vigorous place of interaction between different societies on the face of this planet' (see 'The Sea Between the Lands' on page 13). *Busy*, is how the Mediterranean was described to us at school; people sailing across it back and forth and forth and back, exploring, exchanging, confronting, converging over a complex expanse of water. We learned that what happened on the sea shaped what happened on the land touching it. How that land was shared between civilisations and empires, divided into continents – Africa, Europe and Asia – and, currently, twenty-two countries and one territory: Spain, France, Monaco, Italy, Malta, Slovenia, Bosnia

Cultivation of the vine originated not among the breezes of the Mediterranean but at the foot of the Caucuses, in Georgia, around eight thousand years ago. It then travelled to Mesopotamia before making its way to ancient Greece, where it put down roots and sprang up all along the Mediterranean, a crucial crossroads for trade and culture. From Andalusia to southern France, from Italy to the Balkan coast and as far as Lebanon, Israel and the Greek islands, today Mediterranean viticulture is spread across more than twenty countries with an area under cultivation of around four million hectares, more than half of the world's total. But this winemaking identity is underpinned by a surprising degree of heterogeneity. Rather than expressing a unified Mediterranean, each wine reflects one area, a specific climate, flora and people, all different but symbiotic. The grapes themselves, on this constant journey, speak different languages: Sardinia's cannonau becomes grenache on the French coast, whereas on the Costa Brava it is garnacha; Sicilian insolia is one and the same variety as ansonica on the island of Elba or roditis in the Greek islands; the primitivo grown in Manduria, Puglia – which has even travelled as far as California, where it is called zinfandel – is known as crljenak in Croatia. *Vinum nostrum* conceals an identity built on sea, rock, sun and wind, elements that imbue it with a profile on the palate and nose in which the aromas are often reminiscent of the local scrub and its herbs, and the flavours are sometimes defined by a distinct saline component, aspects that, as well as confirming the correspondence between geography and taste, also encapsulate the many faces of the Mediterranean.

and Herzegovina, Croatia, Montenegro, Albania, Greece, Turkey, Cyprus, Syria, Lebanon, Israel, Palestine, Egypt, Libya, Tunisia, Algeria, Morocco and Gibraltar.

*

In a city that touches the sea, Keys and Haney spent a month in Naples in 1951 with Bergami and his assistant Flaminio Fidanza, working out of a lab at the department of medicine. They focused on examining blood samples from volunteers organised by Bergami: a group of middle-aged men working as firemen and health inspectors. Analysis revealed negligible harmful cholesterol levels. The question 'What did you eat yesterday?' almost always received the same answer: pasta, vegetables, fruit, occasionally a bit of meat and dairy. It was preliminary sketching rather than rigorous research, but one clear enough to fuel Keys's hypothesis about cholesterol and heart disease, food regimes as prevention and to convince the whole team that research into ways of eating, 'diet', was important.

Growing up in England in the 1980s with a mother who was invariably on a diet until she fell off it, I can't shake the narrow idea that diet *only* means quantitative control of weight, waist and calories, how to lose two kilos in two days, fit into your slim-cut jeans again. Then, as a drama student in London in the 1990s, diet meant cold cans of Coke and slogans 'Just for the taste of it'. The word's

'Growing up in England in the 1980s with a mother who was invariably on a diet until she fell off it, I can't shake the narrow idea that diet *only* means quantitative control of weight, waist and calories.'

meaning becomes more explicit when we return to its Greek root, *diaita*, 'way of life', with its designated rules of conduct, which didn't always involve food, that served to guide all sorts of behaviours, from sobriety to opulence. The anthropologist Marino Niola (in *The Secrets of the Mediterranean Diet*, which he co-authored with Elisabetta Moro) goes further with a definition found in ancient literature, in which diet is 'a physical and symbolic place, both physiological and social, where habitual human practices take place'. Niola also observes how the Greek term *diaitao* propels the word into action – 'govern', 'judge', 'discuss' – while the philosopher Martin Heidegger suggests an etymological similarly between *diaita* and the Old High German *buan*, 'to live', and *bin*, 'to be'.

Then there is dietetics, the branch of knowledge concerned with diet and its effects on health, which, according to historian Massimo Montanari, was born with cooking when humans first learned to transform food with fire. A simple act, which from the very beginning was intended to improve taste but also enhance health and hygiene, making the interdependence of dietetics and cooking a given. Over time the Greeks (as was the case with all civilisations) evolved dietetics into medical and philosophical systems rigorously tied to culinary practice. All these meanings are a long way from losing two kilos in two days. For the ancients, diet meant life,

pleasure and health, while for some of us moderns, diet is simply about waist size. (Although surely there have always been those with that goal in mind!)

The next phase of Keys's and Haney's research was in Madrid with Carlos Jiménez Díaz and a group of volunteers from the working-class quarter of Cuatro Caminos. Samples and questions regarding what the men ate revealed similar results to Naples. Thanks to Keys's diary, there are observations, too, about culinary practices and habits, adding context as to *how* people eat and not just *what* they eat. One entry records how eating Spanish tortilla, a dish of potato and egg, at lunchtime could see one through to dinner, which might not start until 11 p.m. and end at 2 a.m. (Keys doesn't attempt to hide his culture shock.)

In 1954 the couple returned to the team in Naples. Again the volunteers were male, between the ages of forty and forty-nine: 150 firemen, 138 steel workers, sixty-eight office workers, along with comparative studies of forty-nine Neapolitan cashiers and bank managers, fifty-four policemen in Bologna and 205 white-collar workers in Minneapolis, USA. Keys and co-authors Fidanza and Scardi added a new observation, physical activity, which produced surprising results: those with the most physically demanding, energy-expending work, steel workers, presented the same low levels of cholesterol as firemen and sedentary workers. Consistency was

seen in food, too, all three groups sharing a similar pattern: large amounts of bread and vegetables, bean dishes at least three times a week, several glasses of wine a day, bits of cheese on pasta and small amounts of meat. Also noted was the use of olive oil, a scant knowledge of butter and that milk was consumed only by children. The result from Minneapolis, however, revealed consistently high levels of cholesterol, leaving Keys even more convinced of an important nexus between cardiovascular diseases and dietary fats. He concluded that

if middle-aged American men ate more like their southern-Italian counterparts they'd have a better chance of not dropping dead from heart attacks.

It is a gentle irony that an element of the Neapolitan diet being advocated, one intimately associated with Italian identity, the tomato, as well as certain varieties of bean, were recent immigrants from America. Also interesting is that pasta and tomato sauce, often made with butter or '*nzogna* (lard), only became common in Naples in the early 1800s. It is fascinating to look at *all* the

elements of what the men ate. They fit neatly into Massimo Montanari's lesson on layers of dynamic cultural exchange: the civilisation of bread and wine born in the regions of the Afro-Asian Near and Middle East; bread, olive oil, wine, lamb and onion part of the ancient Greek and Roman traditions; the culture of pork thanks to the melding of the Roman and the 'barbaric'; artichokes, citrus, aubergine, spinach, sugar and dry pasta brought to Europe by the Arabs during the Middle Ages; the tomatoes, varieties of beans, potatoes and corn that came from America in the modern age. And it continues, every arrival being an opportunity for the integration and assimilation of new products and culinary skills. This isn't intended to diminish 'local food identity' only to expand it and remember that many foods thought of as Mediterranean are not of Mediterranean origin at all, that, like all culinary traditions, the one in Naples came about as a result of endless and ongoing social and cultural intermingling, integration and assimilation.

*

The next stage for the team was long-term research in seven countries. Such an undertaking required methodology, so a pilot study in a small town where life was regular and the population homogenous (and willing to collaborate) was necessary. Alfonso del Vecchio, one of the collaborating professors, suggested his home town of Nicotera in Calabria. In October 1957 Keys and Haney, Mario Mancini of Naples, Vittorio Puddu of Rome, Noboru Kimura of Kyushu, Jack Brock of Cape Town, Martti Karvonen of Helsinki and Christos Aravanis of Athens all assembled in Calabria, staying at the rather hopefully named Jolly Hotel in Gioia Tauro. The methodology developed mixed medicine and objective measurements – blood analysis, electrocardiograms and blood pressure – with anthropology and socio-cultural elements, a survey of activity, meals consumed, food production and supply, taking into account intangible elements, too. This was received by observers as revolutionary, quasi-experimental, maverick.

The Seven Countries Study began in 1958. Groups of adult males enrolled in sixteen cohorts in Italy, Greece, The Netherlands, Japan, Finland, Yugoslavia and the USA, later extending to Crete, Corfu, South Africa and Sardinia. A milestone in research, it was the first multi-country epidemiological study, and it would last fifty years. The published findings filled report after report, but, in short, suggested that the risk of heart attacks and strokes correlated to levels of cholesterol and elevated blood pressure and confirmed that deaths from coronary heart disease in the USA and northern Europe far exceeded those in southern Europe. The principal criticisms filled report after report, too – they still do – with subsequent papers challenging the findings on the basis that countries were selected to fit the hypothesis and the suppression of evidence that sugar is more highly correlated with heart disease than fats. What was unanimously agreed, though, was that the Seven Countries Study provided a new model for multi-country study and cooperation and started a domino effect of research and discussion that would lead to two words being put together – although not quite yet!

In 1959 Keys and Haney (as Margaret Keys) published their first book, *Eat Well and Stay Well*, its long front-cover blurb unequivocal: 'What YOU should know about the latest medical discoveries about how your diet affects your heart, arteries, and blood cholesterol level ... How to select and prepare food for eating pleasure and health, with appetizing recipes and menus combining the latest nutritional knowledge and gourmet satisfaction.' Phew! From science and meal planning, the authors adopt a philosophical tone: 'Good and civilized living, and the intellectual search for lasting satisfaction,' they note, 'is a careful balance between current and future pleasures.' They also summon up the

'The published findings confirmed that deaths from coronary heart disease in the USA and northern Europe far exceeded those in southern Europe.'

ancient world and food model, closely linked to the symbolic products of Greek and Roman culture, bread, wine, oil – a trio tightly wrapped in myth, ritual and representing the virtuous relationship between man and nature – then the Christian model of bread and wine being the Eucharistic emblems of the body and blood, the oil for anointing. Marino Niola introduces a playful idea when he describes the sanctifying of the trio as giving it a religious DOC, a consecrated Denomination of Origin. Could this also be true of the authors? That by introducing bread, wine, oil as not just food but as symbolic, sacred – which, of course, they can be – they were suggesting their work might have a touch of that, too!

The book was a bestseller in the USA, and Keys's work put him on the cover of *Time* magazine's diet-and-health issue in January 1961. The lead article paints a picture of a society in crisis: an abundance of food (and 100 million tons a year of surplus to dispose of) and food excess on the one hand, while on the other people were going to bed hungry; the triumph of vitamin capsules, low-calorie foods and fads; and a mass phenomenon of illness through unhealthy eating habits. 'The public wants to know facts about diet and health,' the article states, going on to say that 'the man most firmly at grips with the problem ... is Ancel Keys'. Keys was already lauded in the USA for his development of the nutritionally complete K-ration for soldiers. The article profiles him and the new ambitious study, pulling together conclusions, including a damningly moralistic take on obesity along with forensic facts about fats. Keys, though, never takes his eye off his number-one concern, the number-one killer: coronary artery disease. And his

answer in the article, as in the book, is simple: 'Eat less fat, meat, fewer eggs and dairy products. Spend more time on fish, chicken, calves' liver, Canadian bacon, Italian food, Chinese food, supplemented by fresh fruits, vegetables and casseroles.' Sensible and expansive advice that met with opposition from members of the US National Dairy Council, not surprisingly, and those with different scientific views. Some detractors still refer to him the man who taught the USA to fear fat. There was also the question of the 'diet industry', the explosion of which was another consequence of abundance and excess – or, rather, a reaction against it in the triumph of the cult of thinness. The Atkins, Eskimo, cabbage soup, Stillman and grapefruit diets all squeaked about good health, but weight loss was the undisputed goal. It's clear that in using the word 'diet' in *Eat Well and Stay Well*, Keys and Haney had 'way of life' in mind, but so much of that was drowned out by the feverish slimming culture of the time.

Meanwhile Ancel Keys and Margaret Haney had no doubts as to the way of life they wanted. Doing their time in southern Italy they had identified Pioppi, a coastal town in the Province of Salerno, as an 'uncontaminated' place where food practices and food culture (that is, ideas, customs, beliefs and social behaviours) resulted in longevity and good health. They bought a villa, named it 'Minnelea' (a blend of Minneapolis and the ancient city of Elea) and moved there in 1966 'to lengthen their lives by 20 years'. Keys would live to a hundred, Haney to ninety-seven.

Again, their diary provides a detailed record of their lives, their deepening, if idealised, knowledge of local ways – and not just of what people ate but

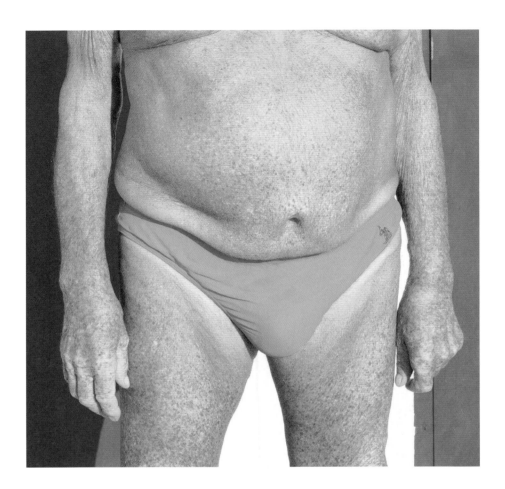

THE MEADOW ON THE SEABED

The French author Georges Duhamel wrote that where the olive trees end the Mediterranean ends. But looking beneath the sea's surface there is another plant that meets the definition, *Posidonia oceanica*, which, in spite of its name, is endemic and exclusive to the Mediterranean. It is a marine plant rather than a type of seaweed, and it forms large underwater meadows that cover around 3 per cent of the entire basin. According to some sources it holds the record as the world's largest living organism with the longest lifespan: in 2006 an individual specimen extending for eight kilometres and estimated to be 100,000 years old was discovered in the Balearics. From the shore, *Posidonia* is often deemed an annoyance because its dead leaves – or banquettes – can wash up and decompose on beaches, but the plant plays a fundamental ecological role in protecting the coast from erosion and offers habitats, food and protection to countless animal and plant species. The plant is also a particularly efficient carbon store, able to absorb fifteen times more

CO_2 than the equivalent area of Amazon rainforest. Because of their complexity and importance, the *Posidonia* beds have been designated a 'priority habitat' and are also used as a bioindicator of the quality of coastal waters, because, as we've come to expect, *Posidonia* meadows are in retreat all across the Mediterranean from the increase in human pressure on coastal areas and the tropicalisation of the sea and with the arrival of harmful invasive species. If he had lived in the 21st century, perhaps Duhamel would have said that when the *Posidonia* ends the Mediterranean will also end.

The Invention of the Mediterranean Diet

how they ate. The word 'Mediterranean' appears more and more regularly. The phrase 'in our Mediterranean' opens a lush description of seasonal produce and their own gardening, how the New Year begins with lemons, oranges and mandarins, while spring brings lettuce, broccoli, fennel, broad beans and tender peas, then summer tomatoes, peppers, aubergines and figs like sweets – no penury, sombre fatalism or violent eruptions here. While another entry explains: 'The Mediterranean for us is made up of about twenty thousand miles of coastline and of four nations, Italy, Greece, the Midi of France, and the Mediterranean coast of Spain.' While the miles suggest the entire twenty-two-country coastline, theirs was an idyllic, sun-drenched, opulent and wholly European 'Med'. But as an English food-writer based in Rome and Sicily, whose work owes much to this abundant and selective view, I am hardly in a position to criticise.

Reductive in some ways, Keys's and Haney's perspective was expanding in others, above all in their belief that in eating for health and longevity, the rituals around food, activity, rest, seasonality and conviviality were every bit as important as the food itself, the results of which manifested in the longevity of the people around them. In 1975 Keys and Haney updated their first book of advice and recipes – and very good and sensible recipes they are, too – to reflect this, lengthening its title to *How to Eat Well and Stay Well the Mediterranean Way*. It is inside the revised edition that the two words 'Mediterranean' and 'diet' are put together for the first time. Elisabetta Moro believes that the couple invented the expression to define the ideal food paradigm, the model to be exported all over the world!

This reduction into a single way is one of the reasons Massimo Montanari finds a definition of Mediterranean diet equivocal, because it suggests the idea of a single diet when geography and history have created 'not one, but many Mediterranean diets', which echoes Fernand Braudel's Mediterranean as 'not a sea, but a succession of seas' (see 'Fernand Braudel' on page 16). Montanari observes that the singular ignores the extreme variety of situations created among such regions as, say Provence and Lebanon, Tunisia, Dalmatia, Sicily and Egypt. Questionable, too, is the presentation of things as a 'simple recovery of olden times', because again it ignores complexity and constant change. The food the Neapolitan men ate in 1950, also the long-living Cilentani, the bread, beans, olive oil, tomatoes, aubergines, pasta, citrus, spinach, grapes, cheese, breakfast *cornetti* and (no doubt) buns filled with custard were, and are, the result of dynamic borrowing, dissemination and appropriation in space and over time, food practices and products from all over the globe. The idea of an 'ideal model' is hugely problematic, too, however good the model is, because it suggests one cultural food tradition is superior to any other. We could also ask questions as to why the Mediterranean diet is the best known and most studied dietary pattern globally – because its great value as a paradigm also has huge economic value.

Again, though, this isn't about diminishing the work of Ancel Keys, Margaret Haney and their colleagues Anna Ferro-Luzzi, Alessandro Menotti, Mario Mancini, Paul White, Antonia Trichopoulou and others. Their collaborative research, in particular the Seven

Countries Study, was fundamental to our understanding the relationship between diet and disease. It also precipitated an avalanche of academic research and clinical studies, as did the diet they mapped, most recognisable as a pyramid, with its base of fruit, vegetables, nuts and cereals and olive oil, moderate amounts of fish, poultry, dairy and wine and small amounts of red meat, processed food and sweets. A 2018 report commissioned by the World Health Organization looked at 4,011 academic articles, 789 conference papers, ten books and policy in fifteen countries and concluded that the Mediterranean diet along with the Nordic diet are the most likely dietary models to provide protection against coronary heart disease as well as cancers, respiratory conditions and diabetes. The Eurocentricity of the research is something to be questioned, however, especially when it is providing the basis for a *global* health policy.

Something agreed upon, though, is that diet is a way of life that involves a set of skills, knowledge, rituals, symbols and traditions concerning crops, harvesting, fishing, animal husbandry, conservation, processing, cooking and, in particular, the sharing of food, and this is how the Mediterranean diet is defined by UNESCO as an Intangible Cultural Heritage of Humanity. And, thankfully, not just one but several Mediterranean diets; seven so far from seven participating countries, each one with an emblematic town or place: Brač and Hvar in Croatia, Agros in Cyprus, Koroni in Greece, Pollica in Italy, Chefchaouen in Morocco, Tavira in Portugal and Soria in Spain. Fifteen countries and one territory to go!

The trolley filled with ingredients that opens this article, is a shopping-list

A NICE DROP OF ANISE

They are not mentioned as part of the Mediterranean diet – nor, indeed, any other diet designed to promote healthy eating – but aniseed-flavoured liqueurs are as much a Mediterranean product as olive oil, common all along the coastline. Like the olive tree, green anise is indigenous to the region, a native of the eastern Mediterranean. The Romans liked to put it in wine, but the key innovation was the addition of sugar and alcohol to create a clear liqueur that takes on a cloudy, milky appearance when you add ice or water (a phenomenon known scientifically as the 'ouzo effect'). Each Mediterranean country has its own version (and often a lot more than one). Greek ouzo, rakı in Turkey and Albania and arak in Lebanon and North Africa are distilled from a base of grapes and aniseed, mastika in the Balkans is made from plums, and then there is anisette, sambuca, pastis, chinchón … In its myriad varieties it is a liqueur with a literary and artistic pedigree almost as rich as the Mediterranean itself: absinthe – its unsweetened cousin – was the drink of the *poètes maudits*, whereas Hemingway's characters drink Anís del Toro; another Spanish drink, Anís del Mono, travelled as far as Mexico in Malcolm Lowry's *Under the Volcano*; Italian anisette made it to Hollywood with Francis Ford Coppola (*The Godfather*) and Martin Scorsese (*Goodfellas*). All over the world, its fresh, sugary taste inevitably conjures up the sound of the waves, the breeze ruffling the sea's surface, the sun going down … and the headache the morning after.

summary inspired by the work of Tunisian historian Yassine Essid. In his expansive essay on the history of Mediterranean food he, too, recognises not one but *many* Mediterranean diets but also asks a question: could a coherent model of Mediterranean food common to all the surrounding countries and recognisable to a Mediterranean dweller be derived from such a variety of cultures and religious beliefs? His answer is yes, but in order to find the model it's necessary to reconstruct the history of Mediterranean food, and the best way to do

that is to go shopping with a local. It is a metaphysical shop of great detail, navigating geographical, mutual and religious differences and the vicissitudes of history. Farming with Sumerians, at sea with Phoenicians, sheep farming in Egypt and Libya, chatting to ancient Greek and Roman cooks, making field trips to the Maghreb and Mexico, drinking tea in Tunisia, meeting shopkeepers from Persia, India, Syria, gossiping about Ottoman cuisine and the Sabbath. It is the back and forth and forth and back we were taught at school in edible

detail, culminating in a true blending of cultures and a very full trolley.

Wheat, barley, spelt, peas, lentils, chickpeas, broad beans, olive oil, cardoons, chard, purslane, lettuce, endives, asparagus, carrots, garlic, onions, turnips, celery, cabbages, pomegranates, quinces, almonds, pistachios, dates, figs, grapes, vine leaves, honey, goats, beef, sheep, poultry, eggs, milk, cheese, butter, salt, game, deer, antelopes, gazelles, wild boar, grasses, roots, tubers, seeds, pears, apples, walnuts, hazelnuts, chestnuts, date palms, fish, shellfish and crustaceans, citrus fruits, rice, sugar, pasta, spinach, aubergines, cocoa, chocolate, sorghum, millet, couscous, carob, jujubes, limes, citrons, peaches, apricots, plums, cherries, azaroles, medlars, whitecurrants and blackcurrants, green beans, peas, cauliflowers, cucumbers, melons and water melons, cumin, caraway and aniseed, henna, saffron, oregano, myrtle, jasmine, roses, narcissi, water lilies, goldenrod, wallflowers, marjoram, violets, lilies, thyme, opium poppies and Indian hemp, pepper, cloves, ginger, nutmeg, cassia,

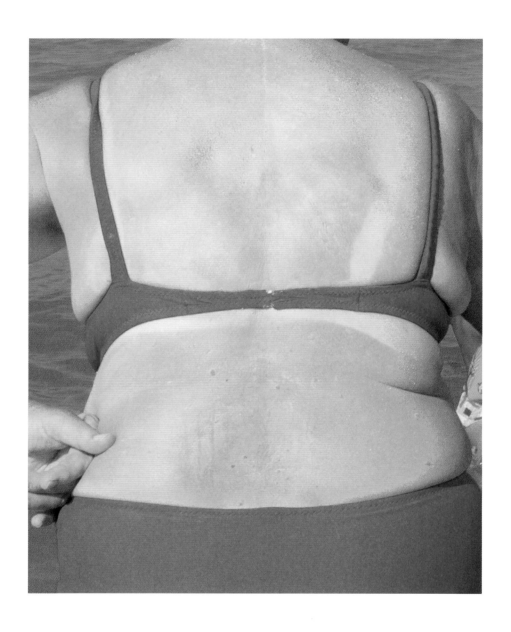

'Eating together is the foundation of the cultural identity and continuity of communities throughout the Mediterranean Basin.'

manna, rhubarb, aloes, gum, maize, tomatoes, potatoes, peppers, prickly pears, beans, squash, myrtle, paprika, new types of olives, coffee, tea.

The beauty of the list is in the way it shows how many things could be made in how many different ways. Essid also comes to the conclusion that, as well as shared products reconfigured in thousands of ways, eating together is the foundation of the cultural identity and continuity of communities throughout the Mediterranean Basin and that time taken and the social practices of conviviality are what really unite. 🐦

One Face,
One Race

Translated by Kate Ferguson
Photographs are from the author's collection

Zülfü Livaneli

In the Aegean and the eastern Mediterranean Greece and Turkey have been at daggers drawn since the Greek War of Independence two centuries ago. But, according to one great Turkish writer and musician who has made himself the living embodiment of the message of friendship and peace between the two countries, what unites the two peoples runs much deeper than what separates them – and this comes to the fore in times of great need.

93

Akdeniz Akdeniz, senden aslımız
Masmavi bir aydınlıktan gelir neslimiz

Mediterranean, oh Mediterranean, you are the source of our essence
A deep-blue light our generation's provenance

Zülfü Livaneli, 'Akdeniz Akdeniz'

The Mediterranean, music and a shared history. These three things have been behind the most meaningful work I have undertaken in my life. The concert at the Ariston Theatre in Sanremo the day I received the Tenco Prize, the first song I sang with Melina Mercouri in front of the town hall in Marseilles, the unforgettable concerts with Maria del Mar Bonet in Majorca, Barcelona and Istanbul and, of course, in Greece, which I count as my second country. That country with whose people we share an embrace, with whose musicians we share our lives, our sorrows, our music. The enthusiasm borne from the many collaborations, starting with Maria Farantouri and Mikis Theodorakis. The concert at the ancient theatre in Ephesus with Theodorakis and Manos Hadzidakis, where the candles held by the thirty thousand spectators seemed to reach to the stars.

Like all peoples of the Mediterranean, the Greeks have suffered and have turned their suffering into eternal joy in the songs they sing. They are aware of the serious work they are doing. A meditation

ZÜLFÜ LIVANELI is a Turkish musician, novelist, journalist and film director. He is the author of twenty-one novels (five of which – *Bliss, Serenade for Nadia, Disquiet, The Last Island* and, most recently, *The Fisherman and His Son* – have been published in English) and has released around fifty albums. He has collaborated with dozens of international artists including Mikis Theodorakis, Joan Baez and Maria Farantouri and has written the soundtrack for a number of films including *Yol*, directed by Şerif Gören and Yilmaz Güney, which was awarded the Palme d'Or at Cannes in 1982. He has long been active in Turkish political life – taking liberal, pacifist and multicultural positions – and has worked extensively to promote dialogue and friendship between Turks and Greeks. He has been a **UNESCO** Goodwill Ambassador since 1995.

on life, death, the world and creation. The song is like the moment of revelation of one of mortal humankind's tragic secrets. It is a ceremonial rite, a ritual sacrifice, yet what flows from the wounds is not blood but the strains of a dusky voice.

I was surprised when I first heard that the Greek word for song is *tragoudi*. There is nothing about the word that makes you think of music. It was later that I made the connection: *tragoudi* comes from the ancient Greek *tragoidia*, 'tragedy'. Making that connection explained a lot.

Through the plastic, multicoloured, candy-pop music of recent years, the capitalist system has attempted to create a host of happy, healthy, dynamic and unthinking workers. Despite this, the entire Mediterranean – from Sicily to Crete and from Barcelona to Mersin – rings with songs that echo with a tragic melancholy.

Yet the melancholy of the Mediterranean is different from that of other regions. The song of the Mediterranean is not a howl. It is not like arabesque – a style I have always found to be foreign, extraneous – which exudes an obsession with death fuelled by anger and destruction as it cries, 'Look at the state I am in. Have pity on me. Let's all weep together and curse life,' because, according to the philosopher Erich Fromm, an obsession with death represents a return to the earth and to the mother's womb. The sea, on the other hand, turns suffering into a luminous phosphorescence, burns it with its salt, heals it and returns it to strength. And while the Mediterranean dances along to her song, she says, 'That's just the way it is. Humankind is mortal! We suffer and then leave this beautiful world without ever getting our fill of it. So let's transform this into a great joy in which people stand together, shoulder to shoulder.'

And so, in the words that fall from the lips of the singer, joy and melancholy, suffering and happiness meld into one, recreating humankind and history. The howl of arabesque reflects the desire of the peasant, newly arrived in the city, to begin a life filled with wealth and beautiful women; the song of the Mediterranean, on the other hand, reflects the melancholy of a philosopher.

One day, in a house on the Greek coast, fifteen or twenty of us were sitting around a table. We were singing folk songs. Then came the

time for the song 'İzmir'in Kavakları', 'The Poplars of Izmir'. Sitting behind me was a group of old Greek women; they must have been ninety years old, perhaps even a hundred. I noticed that one of them, a lady so old her face had turned into the ruins of Ephesus, had a tear running down each cheek. In Turkish, she said, 'I am from Izmir. I had five siblings. The Germans shot all of them. The youngest sang songs like you. His voice was just like yours.'

What remains of that time in Greece are memories made of salt, of retsina, of rebetiko. And also of the prayers of happiness offered to all Turks and all Greeks by an old man at the Papagiannakos family home one evening as he observed the custom of offering the first piece of the traditional Vasilopita cake to the principal male guest as he wished us all *chronia polla*, happy new year.

CRETE

After a concert in Athens an elderly, well-dressed lady from Istanbul came up to me. 'Tell me, do you also put the works of Ahmet

Haşim Bey to music?' she asked, referring to the great 20th-century Turkish poet. 'I'm related to him.' There are many such surprising moments that reveal to us just how intertwined the histories of the two countries are.

Some time later Maria Farantouri and I were touring various cities in Greece. Our 1981 itinerary took in the islands of Crete, Samos, Lesbos, Corfu and Kythira. We held seven concerts in different cities on Crete. When we arrived on the island by plane there were two buses waiting. One of them was for us, along with the members of the eight-piece orchestra and the journalists who were accompanying us, and the other was loaded up with the sound equipment. When a beach took our fancy we would stop and swim in the sea. We would have lunches at fish restaurants on the coast that would last at least three hours. Around tables loaded with red mullet, calamari, lobster, octopus, *horta* (a Cretan speciality) and retsina, we would fall deep into conversation.

After arriving in a city at some point in the afternoon we would stop off at the hotel and then, within an hour at most, head to the venue for a soundcheck. The concerts were generally held in the city's stadium. We would check the sound and lighting and then wait for the concert to begin.

It would be past midnight by the time we finished, and afterwards the mayor and leading figures of the city would host us at the best tavernas in the area. Fifty or sixty people would be at the meals, and, after the official speeches, glasses were raised to Turkish–Greek friendship. As was Greek tradition, at the end of the meal Maria and I would be offered a gift as a souvenir of the occasion. Prayer beads made of seashells on a silver chain or gold-plated leaves like those handmade by the elderly chemist-mayor of Lesbos.

Wherever we went on Crete we would come across traces of the Ottomans. The biggest influence could be seen in Chania, where the Turkish baths still stood and the streets still bore the names of Ottoman pashas. In my mind Crete is synonymous with Nikos Kazantzakis. Even before I had ever seen the island, from his work I knew those monasteries, those black-robed, moustachioed men with prayer beads, the view over the blue sea from forests filled with the sound of thousands of insects under a hot sun. What struck me most about Kazantzakis was his passionate love for his country. That's why, during a press conference in 1980, I spoke to around forty Greek journalists about the writer and how his books had been published in Turkey. They greeted my words somewhat coolly. Later, when I tried to discover why, I was met with the same response from the people I asked. They weren't so fond of Kazantzakis. I learned the reason later, and trusted Greek friends confirmed my conclusions.

Kazantzakis was an honourable man. He would stand up against anything, absolutely anything that he believed was wrong. As Fellini said, there was no one who could think in his place. And, because he spoke his mind, people didn't like him. Not the government, not the opposition, not the other parties. Amid this polarised atmosphere, where everybody had to choose their tribe, Kazantzakis was alone. He was a member of no one's team; he rented out his mind to no one.

But was it only Kazantzakis who experienced this? Many 20th-century intellectuals shared a similar fate. Some killed themselves. Some, like Kazantzakis, went into voluntary exile. Some were accused of being traitors, turncoats. These intellectuals were persecuted by governments and castigated by the opposition, unable to reap the rewards of their great minds.

One of these was Heinrich Böll, liked by nobody but his readers. Despite being a Catholic he refused to pay the controversial German tax to the Catholic Church and spoke out against the Church gaining too much power, ultimately leaving in protest. Since he opposed the right, he was attacked by the chancellor with the fiercest of insults. In the 20th century primitive hordes still living in intellectual caves burned down his house. Most leftist groups and parties criticised him for not following their party line. Böll witnessed all of this with melancholy eyes as the contours of his face drooped in sorrow.

Another intellectual who shared such a fate was Antonio Gramsci. His warnings about Mussolini were ignored. His theory that fascism had, for the first time in history, found a way to rally the petite bourgeoisie – something that was to change the course of the century – was passed over without being given any real consideration. Mussolini, on the other hand, did not fail to recognise this most important intellectual threat against him and made sure to destroy him.

LIKE A BIRD OF PREY

In Crete we were followed by a German television crew for the channel ZDF, filming for the cultural programme *Aspekte*. They recorded the concerts in Agios Nikolaos, Anogia and Chania and interviewed Maria and I. Anogia is a hillside town on the slopes of Mount Ida, the highest mountain in Crete, and, during the concert at the town's Xylouris Theatre, the television crew also spoke to members of the audience. One of their interviewees was an elderly man with hair and beard of pure white. He was dressed traditionally and looked the picture of health for his eighty-one years.

'Why did you come here this evening?'

'Because there's a Turk here.'

'Do you like the Turks?'

'No. I fought them. We killed each other's families.'

'Then why did you come?'

'For two reasons. First, the Turks sing so beautifully and, second, ... well ...' The old man paused before asking the journalist, 'Are you German?'

'Yes!'

'Then you wouldn't understand!'

When this conversation was later broadcast on German television the Germans were very moved. This complex relationship was something they were not familiar with.

After the concert the old man came backstage. He looked like a bird of prey. He was mad with excitement and stammered as he spoke. He asked me a question. 'What did he say?' I asked. They interpreted for me. It turns out he was saying, 'Is your name Mustafa, too?' (He must have been thinking of Mustafa Kemal Atatürk!)

That evening the mayor invited us to a mountain restaurant for a meal of roast goat. Something had been preying on my mind. Some of the concerts were in regions that had been under Turkish rule for hundreds of years. Others, such as Corfu or Kythira, were places where the Turks had never set foot. They had never fought the Turks, never lived under Turkish rule and therefore, I had assumed, would be more friendly towards us. But, in fact, the opposite was the case. In those places my songs were listened to with a calm enjoyment, much in the way they would be by any European audience. Those who had lived alongside the Turks, on the other hand, were beside themselves with enthusiasm at the concerts. Perhaps they were overcome with a nostalgic thrill, as though searching for their own past. It seems that even the worst of relationships is better than no relationship at all. From this I reached the following conclusion: the average European is further from Turkey than the average Greek.

Over the course of history the peoples of the south have shared the same fate, and they formed great civilisations at times when human relations and richness of character held importance. Later, in the industrial period – a time that required a workforce that was transformed into abstract labour and when human relationships became worthless – they lost their power, their supremacy falling to northern Protestants. Now they look upon the technical superiority and social organisation of the north in awe, yet they continue to go about their lives following their own traditions based on human relationships, shared customs and friendship.

ALL THE DIGNIFIED PEOPLE OF TURKEY AND GREECE

1 July 1981 … We were heading to a concert in Missolonghi. Everyone – our manager Manthos, Vera, Maria, the members of the orchestra – was a little on edge. When we reached the city, I understood why.

I left our hotel, the Liberty, to go for a short walk. Three-hundred metres away was a park filled with white statues. They were the statues of Greeks who died fighting the Turks. In the final battle thirteen thousand Greek soldiers are said to have perished. Missolonghi is also where Lord Byron died. The city is known for keeping the memory of the war alive. A conservative, fanatical place.

We were waiting in the bus that was parked behind the stage in the middle of the stadium. The stalls were getting fuller by the minute. 'You'll see,' said Maria. 'I have always trusted my people.' That's what she said, but she also had her doubts. 'If we want to put an end

One Face, One Race

to enmity, there are certain risks we have to take.'

I agreed with her. As the concert started the crowd was buzzing. Below the projectors that shone towards the stage I could see thousands of insects fluttering in the air. The heat stuck to our skin like a wet shirt. The running order was the same as always, and after the closing bars of Theodorakis's 'March of the Spirit' Maria announced, 'Our next guest is a Turkish composer ...' and the crowd erupted. I walked out on to the stage. I looked at Maria. She stood there in her red dress, joy on her face, her eyes sparkling. Isn't this exactly why we do this? To feel this emotion, to taste the inimitable joy of peace.

As the orchestra struck up, the crowd clapped along in time. In front of me was an expanse of darkness. I couldn't see the audience, but I could sense their attentive interest like the breath of a giant. It was as though in front of me were not the people of Missolonghi but honourable Turks and Greeks who, through the various schemes of external forces, had been turned against each other, made to believe they were enemies, their lives needlessly squandered. We played a song in 5/8 rhythm ... they clapped along in time, never missing a beat. A 9/8 rhythm, the same. We moved to a 7/8 rhythm, they still kept perfect time. This is the proof of the musical bond between the two countries. (I can't say the same thing for the lyrics, of course.)

After the concert Manthos said to me, 'You are the first Turk to come here since the war.'

FIRE IN ATHENS

The tour of Greece was interrupted by an invitation from Fidel Castro. Mikis and Maria headed to Cuba for ten days. We stayed in Maria's house, waiting for the second half of the tour.

On 4 August, towards the afternoon, the air began to fill with the smell of smoke. The smell of burning wood … The temperature started to rise. I went out into the garden to see what was happening. The flames were heading towards us. We hosed everything down until the fire reached the trees. As the flames licked the edge of the garden, Maria's upstairs neighbour, Angelo, yelled, 'Come on, we need to get out of here.'

We ran into the house to grab our money and passports. And the dogs, too: Surabaya, Doggie, Mando, Vubale … Four dogs. They were wild with fear. The street was filled with fire engines and police officers giving the order to evacuate.

The owner of the house next door jumped into his car, one of his dogs beside him. He put his foot on the accelerator and raced off. His Doberman, who he always kept in the garden, ran after him. A very elderly woman dressed in black was standing in the middle of the road in shock. We crammed into the car: Angelo, Helen, my wife Ülker, my daughter Aylin, me and the four dogs … Maria's huge white Labrador Surabaya was on my lap, out of her mind with fear. She was lashing out at anything and everything. 'Wouldn't it be ironic,' I thought to myself, 'if she went mad from fear and ripped us all to pieces.'

As the flames began to surround us we started to move off. The old woman was still rooted to the spot in the middle of the road. We grabbed her by the arm and pulled her into the crowded car. The whole area was being evacuated. We left Maria's Citroën parked outside the house. We didn't have the key. As the flames engulfed the car, it exploded.

After a while we dropped the old woman off and carried on to the centre of Athens, at least twenty-five kilometres from the fire. A sheet of black smoke covered the sky, soot rained down from above. We were all deeply worried.

Angelo said, 'That's life.' Angelo, the architect of the building, lived with his American wife Helen on the top floor. He had given years of his life to constructing the most beautiful house in Athens only to lose it after having lived there just five or six months. It can't have been easy. But, despite everything, they tried to keep smiles on their faces and not let it get to them. Three hours later we decided to go back to see how things were. The main roads were closed, so we took the back roads to get to the house.

The whole area was completely scorched. The forest, the trees, the grass – anything that had been green just that morning – were black as coal. Water was dripping from every corner of the house. Maria's navy-blue Citroën was nothing but a white tin shell. The house was still standing, but its blinds were drooping, its windows broken, and a smell of smoke had impregnated everything.

Throughout the night the fire continued. We watched on from a distant house in Athens and could see the red flames grow more intense as they spread. Most Greeks were overcome by a kind of mystical fear, as though they had been struck by the wrath of a mythological god. At the same time they knew that fires that had started in different parts of the city could not be a coincidence. The date was also telling: 4 August – the anniversary of the day Metaxas declared his dictatorship in 1936.

It was later understood – from those who were arrested and from other evidence – that this was the work of groups connected to the Regime of the Colonels, the leaders of which were in prison. They called themselves the Blue Archers. For some reason all terrorist organisations have a penchant for romantic names like this. Isn't one of the armed groups that has caused such bloodshed in Turkey called the Mobilisation of Hearts? The rise in terror attacks is directly proportional to the importance of public opinion. In order to influence that now essential force known as public opinion (to strike fear, to intimidate, to win over, to cause panic, to undermine trust in the government ...) all kinds of terror attacks were taking place. In other words, if public opinion didn't matter, terrorism would not, for the most part, exist. We can see this in the hundreds of innocent people who have been killed simply to scare the public and create a power vacuum. When balanced, right-minded people are attacked, a part of everyone is killed, because these people are not, to follow the commonplace logic, 'those who live by the sword'. They represent the public. It is not them as individuals who are attacked, but the institutions they represent. The attack on Pope John Paul II by the Turk Mehmet Ali Ağca was an attempt to implement this on an even larger scale.

Throughout my life I have tried to emphasise the Mediterranean identity of Turkey, a country squeezed between the Balkans, the Middle East and the Caucasus and with a complex history in all these areas. Because the identity that will cleanse us is that of the world's most beautiful continent – the sixth continent – the civilisation of the Mediterranean.

EARTHQUAKES KNOW NO BORDERS
It is not only shared history and culture that unites Turkey and Greece but also geography. Just like the songs, the food, the folk tales and epics, the fault lines that run beneath us never ask for a passport; the earthquakes that occasionally strike both countries remind us, whatever our nationality, of the true nature of our existence as a mammal in nature, not the false identity given by chance as a result of the place we were born. Because when the earthquake strikes, it asks no one for their name, nationality or religion. And when earthquakes remind the peoples of both countries of this basic truth, feelings of solidarity grow, because it is at those times that

our existence as humans comes to the fore, in all its frailty and all its magnificence.

We witnessed this once again in the earthquake that struck the east of Turkey in 2023. Following this horrendous event, in which tens of thousands of people lost their lives, Greece, like the rest of the world, rushed to our aid. Greek search-and-rescue teams brought tears to the eyes of the millions watching on their television screens as they tearfully embraced the children and adults they pulled from the rubble. The same had happened after the 1999 earthquake. When Greece rushed to Turkey's aid and sent food and medical supplies, it swelled the hearts of people on both sides and accelerated initiatives aimed at building friendship.

Mikis Theodorakis and I held solidarity concerts in Greece, Turkey and various European cities to help those who had suffered. But in Athens something interesting happened. On the day of the concert, as if to highlight the artificial nature of national borders, there was an earthquake in the city.

That morning Mikis and I, together with the Turkish, German and Greek musicians, held our last rehearsal. When we went to the restaurant for lunch it was almost three o'clock. We had just sat down and were studying the menu when the trembling started, accompanied by an incredible roar. The restaurant was on the ground floor of a fifteen-storey building. That huge block began to tremble like a leaf. I had experienced that shaking in Istanbul, that roaring sound as if the doors of hell had opened, that boiling of the earth. As soon as I felt the first vibrations I threw myself under the table – all those programmes about what to do in an earthquake broadcast on TV back home must have sunk in – and I wrapped my arms around my head as I waited for that terrible moment to pass.

I can say that I felt that earthquake as strongly as I had in Istanbul, perhaps even more so, but the fact that it only lasted between ten and fifteen seconds saved Athens from a major disaster. Terrible screams came from the restaurant. Images of the earthquake in Turkey must have had an impact, and people were running around in panic. I saw a man kick out a pane of glass so he could escape through the window. As soon as the quake was over we ran outside. A cloud of dust covered the streets. Cars had been left abandoned in the middle of the road, many with their doors open.

In central Athens, even in areas where the buildings were new and well constructed, the streets were filled with debris. There were even cracks in the huge, majestic hotels next to the parliament building in the city's famous Syntagma Square.

What followed would be familiar to anyone who had experienced the earthquake in Turkey. First, everyone turned to their phones, but, just as in Turkey, the aftermath of the earthquake brought problems with the communications systems. Everyone descended on the parks and squares, and with every aftershock people would run around in panic. The evening brought more tremors, some of them very strong, and the people of Athens were truly terrified. Just like in Istanbul, they prepared to spend the night outdoors.

Our solidarity concert that evening was, of course, cancelled. And this time it was rescue teams from Turkey who rushed to help.

One moment that I will never forget was my meeting in a hotel in Athens with Yanni, who had written to me personally to say that he wanted to donate a kidney to an earthquake survivor in Turkey. Yanni was a calm-natured man, a civil servant on a middling income. He told me that on seeing all the injured people on television he wondered what he could do to help and had decided to donate a kidney.

Stefan Zweig said that there are certain moments in human history when we see shooting stars, historical moments that 'outshine the past'. I see those stars of humanity in the solidarity between Greece and Turkey when earthquakes hit. ✒

Mediterranean EEZs

According to the United Nations Convention on the Law of the Sea, every country has the right to an Exclusive Economic Zone that can extend up to 200 nautical miles (370 kilometres) from its coastline. But in the Mediterranean maritime boundaries are very often much closer than that. In the Strait of Sicily, for instance, Italy, Malta, Tunisia and Libya's EEZs would inextricably overlap, so the Mediterranean nations have traditionally opted not to created them. But in the 1990s things began to change: the first nation to create a reserved fishing zone was Algeria, while the EU subsequently pushed for the establishment of protected zones for Spain, France, Italy and Croatia, with the aim of tackling illegal fishing by non-Mediterranean boats. In 2021 the Italian parliament approved a law authorising the establishment of a genuine EEZ.

A Greek island in a Turkish sea

The island of Kastellorizo (Megisti) – population 549, according to the 2021 census – is connected to the rest of the world by a small airport that sees four flights a week and a port where a ferry brings in a few dozen day-trippers during summer from the neighbouring Turkish town of Kaş, three kilometres away. The nearest part of Greece is Rhodes, 125 kilometres to the west, but according to Greece, Kastellorizo has the right to its own EEZ, a wedge within the territorial shelf claimed, not entirely unreasonably, by Turkey. Complicating the matter is the division of Cyprus: the Turkish Republic of Northern Cyprus and its EEZ are recognised only by Turkey, which nevertheless maintains that islands are not entitled to an exclusive zone extending beyond their territorial waters (twelve nautical miles, or twenty-two kilometres, from the coast). Turkey's activism is in line with its 'Blue Homeland' doctrine, developed in 2006, which is based on the modernisation of its navy and a redrawing of the maritime areas from which Turkey was excluded following the First World War.

OPEC for gas

What shook things up was the discovery of gas in the eastern Mediterranean. The first deposits, the Tamar and Leviathan fields, were discovered off the coast of Israel, followed by Zohr in Egyptian waters (the largest site ever discovered in the Mediterranean, large enough to make Egypt potentially self-sufficient) then Calypso and Aphrodite around Cyprus, where, in 2022, ENI and TotalEnergies announced the discovery of Cronos, another immense field. The US Geological Survey estimates that there are 8,000 billion cubic metres'-worth of reserves yet to be discovered in the Levantine Sea, a treasure trove that is redrawing balances and alliances: in 2019 the East Mediterranean Gas Forum was formed by Cyprus, Egypt, Greece, Israel, Jordan, the Palestinian Authority, Italy and France, a sort of Mediterranean OPEC for gas, from which Turkey was excluded. Gas has shuffled the deck for Israel, giving it unexpected leverage for cooperation with Egypt and Jordan (which has already started to receive gas from the Leviathan field) and even an agreement with Hezbollah to renegotiate the contested maritime boundary with Lebanon. For its part, Turkey has worked with Libya to redefine their respective areas of jurisdiction and begun various exploratory projects in contested waters, even sending in the navy to block those of other countries.

EastMed

The challenge now is to bring all that gas to Europe. In 2013 the EastMed project was established as a joint venture between the Italian and Greek utility firms Edison and DEPA to build an underwater gas pipeline linking the Leviathan and Aphrodite fields to Greece and Europe via Cyprus and Crete. However, in 2022 the USA withdrew its support (a concession to its NATO ally Turkey), and the pipeline could be diverted through Egypt to circumvent Cyprus. Whatever happens, it will take years and huge sums of money to build what would be the world's longest undersea gas pipeline. To date liquefication has been the solution, but Egypt has only two regasification plants on the Mediterranean coast, the only ones in the area, which even at maximum capacity could satisfy just 2 per cent of European demand.

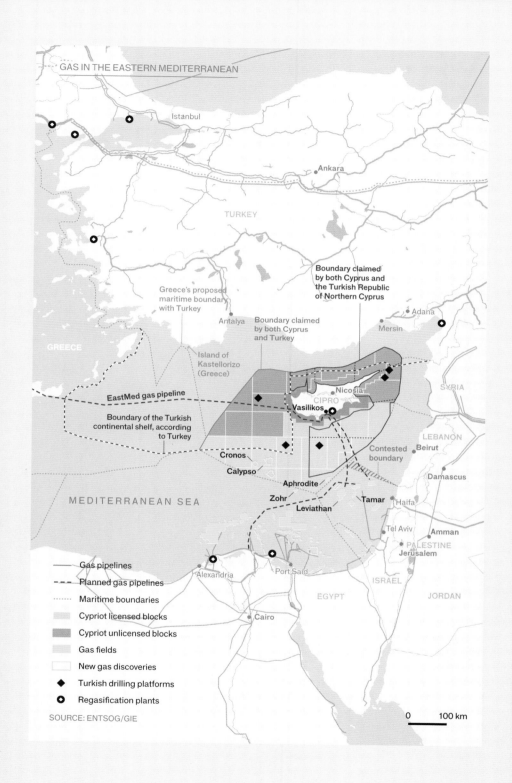

GAS IN THE EASTERN MEDITERRANEAN

Istanbul

Ankara

TURKEY

Boundary claimed
by both Cyprus and
the Turkish Republic
of Northern Cyprus

Adana

Greece's proposed
maritime boundary
with Turkey

Antalya

Mersin

Boundary claimed
by both Cyprus
and Turkey

Island of
Kastellorizo
(Greece)

SYRIA

EastMed gas pipeline

Nicosia

CIPRO

Vasilikos

Boundary of the Turkish
continental shelf, according
to Turkey

LEBANON

Contested
boundary

Beirut

Cronos

Calypso

Damascus

Aphrodite

Zohr

Tamar

Haifa

Leviathan

MEDITERRANEAN SEA

Tel Aviv

Amman

PALESTINE
Jerusalem

Alexandria

Port Said

ISRAEL

JORDAN

EGYPT

Cairo

- Gas pipelines
-- Planned gas pipelines
··· Maritime boundaries
  Cypriot licensed blocks
  Cypriot unlicensed blocks
  Gas fields
  New gas discoveries
◆ Turkish drilling platforms
◉ Regasification plants

SOURCE: ENTSOG/GIE

0   100 km

My Mediterranean

HYAM YARED
Translated by Jennifer Higgins
Photography by Tamara Saade

Raised next to a sea that, following the civil war in Lebanon, represented the possibility of escape but also an impassable barrier, the writer Hyam Yared learned to shift her perspective and turn maps upside down, holding on to the idea that war and peace depend on how we imagine the world – the legacy of a grandmother who was strongly opposed to the prevailing mood of nationalism and sectarianism in recent decades.

111

Below the house in which I grew up on the Christian-militia-controlled hill of Haret Sakher was the sea. There were two railway carriages, which had been devoured by couch grass and rust, sitting side by side next to rails that were covered over by moss and tall grass. The dizzying view from my window over the port of Jounieh made me feel as though I lived in an ocean liner that was ready to launch into the sea. When I woke up, when I went to bed, there was the horizon, taunting me. Indelible. I'd never be allowed to explore it. That was something I'd learn in time. The well-brought-up girls of the family don't travel. Don't aspire to leave. They go to mass on Sundays, that's allowed. To swimming lessons. Assiduously. Obsessively. Two kilometres of breaststroke at my mother's insistence. Crawl, too. In the Olympic pool. Sometimes in the sea. We alternated. She wanted to see my hips disappear. Slimming. Gaining no weight. In the end I became bulimic. A little like this country, as small as a toad but seeing itself as an ox in the midst of a herd of gigantic neighbours. Predation is rarely an idea that enters a child's head. An intuition in a conversation. A gesture. I was slim then. Hips as narrow as the Strait of Gibraltar, which a swimming instructor dreamed of widening without really daring to do so. When predatory behaviour flirts with the art of slowness, we call it abuse. When the gloves are off it becomes rape, invasion, the obliteration of the being by territorial destruction. In either case, it makes us prey. At six, eight and twelve years old, I had no way of imagining the links that could exist between bodies and territory, between this pile of abandoned metal and the history of the great cities of the eastern coastline of this Mediterranean Basin, midway between north and south, like a placenta in the earth's lower belly. From one side the sea called us and from the other the remains of a railway network reminded us that it was no longer possible to travel into what was left of a territory now parcelled up into regions as separate from one another as the hostages of rival militias. It was ten years now since civil war had broken out. It was 1985.

Settled now near this port, to which we'd moved to escape Beirut and its suburbs, we didn't have many options. Leave or stay. 'You don't choose to leave Lebanon,' my mother would say, 'you run away from it.' The bay of Jounieh was the embodiment of this. Throughout my childhood I saw Lebanese people – Christians mostly – flock to the docks, waiting to board ships bound for Limassol, just a fifteen-minute flight from Lebanon, which would have been an ideal distance if our only airport in West Beirut had been accessible. A demarcation line had cut the city in two. Risking

HYAM YARED is a francophone Lebanese writer born in Beirut. Her first collection of poems, *Reflets de lune* (Dar An-Nahar, 2001), won gold at the Jeux de la Francophonie; her second collection, *Blessures de l'eau* (Dar An-Nahar, 2004), also earned many awards. She is the author of several novels – including *Sous la tonnelle* (Sabine Wespieser, 2009), *La malédiction* (Équateurs, 2012) and *Implosions* (Équateurs, 2021) – and her work was included in the *Beirut Noir* collection published in English by Akashic in 2015. She is founder and president of the Lebanese PEN Centre.

TAMARA SAADE is a Lebanese journalist and photographer based in Beirut and New York. Her work primarily takes a documentary approach to Lebanon's ever-changing political landscape, with a particular focus on human rights, through photography, writing and videography. She has worked with, among others, *The New York Times*, *The Washington Post*, *VICE International*, the *Delacorte Review*, *Megaphone*, Al Jazeera and the United Nations and has exhibited in the USA, France, the UAE, Norway and Lebanon.

your life in a game of Russian roulette would have given you better odds than crossing that line. The only option for Lebanese people wanting to find viable peace elsewhere was the port of Jounieh, one night's sail from Cyprus – the insular neighbour that has never lost its status as a promised land ever since the sadly infamous night of 13 April 1975 when the fighting spread out its tentacles. Later, a bus peppered with bullet holes: the starting gun had been fired for community resentment against a background of regional disagreements fed by the internal struggles of a country too young – 'too plural', added Evelyne, my paternal grandmother in whose house we had taken refuge – to impose its sovereignty and rein in those who were benefiting from slowing its development and fuelling its divisions from within, divisions that were manifestations of intrigues murkier than any seabed.

*

Evelyne, whose grey eyes had witnessed this country's identity crises, described the various stages of its existence: from the idea of an autonomous Mount Lebanon that had begun under the Ottoman Empire through the alliance of the Druze and Maronite communities to its emergence as a young nation in the wake of the First World War, as conceived by local dignitaries but also by a victorious Europe keen to wield influence over the territories of the vanquished Ottomans. This

bloody period of the 20th century, and the replacement of imperial, monarchical and colonial visions with the emergence of nation states, was deplored by Evelyne as the cause of the decline of that diversity of which the Ottoman Mount Lebanon and contemporary Lebanon had boasted, wrongly, as she said. 'Wrongly!' She railed against the 'Lebanisation' of this diversity by those who didn't look beyond their own noses to the wider sweep of history. She went right back to the ancient civilisations to demonstrate that the world, in a broad sense, is such a crucible of millennia-old exchanges that there could be no Lebanon-specific diversity any more than there was a Mediterranean diversity. It was, in her eyes, part of the way of the world since Cain and Abel, since Moses, of people torn between nomadism and settled life, no matter what conflicts they were obliged to flee. When I was old enough to argue with her, I pointed out the anachronism of her examples. Almost all of them were based in this eastern part of the Mediterranean.

*

Above her bed my grandmother had pinned a map of the world upside down, and I never knew if this was her own idea or if it was inspired by Stuart McArthur's flipped map, the Universal Corrective Map of the World. It was difficult to imagine how, in wartime, she might have been aware of the

THE SUICIDE OF A STATE

If the situation in Lebanon was not so tragic it might on some level be almost comic. In 2022, for example, almost all the staff in the country's vehicle registration office were arrested for corruption and never replaced, which means that the roads are increasingly filled with vehicles without licence plates and drivers without licences. Or another example: for three days in March 2023 Lebanese citizens had clocks showing different times because Muslims unilaterally delayed the changing of the clocks to wait for the end of Ramadan. Of course, this is still better than shooting at each other, as was the case during the civil war that devastated the country between 1975 and 1990, but in 2020 the accidental explosion of 2,750 tonnes of ammonium nitrate stored in unsafe conditions in the Port of Beirut – which killed more than two hundred people, injured thousands more and destroyed over half of the country's grain reserves – demonstrated that neglect, corruption and impunity can do just as much damage. The fragile peace of 1990 re-established the so-called 'national pact' under which the functions of the state are divided between the religious faiths according to quotas – a solution that preserves national unity but at the price of crystallisation of divisions and the creation of fiefdoms that parcel up the country's wealth. The result is a constant and profound crisis: GDP more than halved between 2019 and 2021, 80 per cent of the population live below the poverty line and public services are paralysed. And the sea here is not only a much-needed source of tourism income but has become an escape route – as well as an ever more crowded cemetery, much as elsewhere in the Mediterranean.

work of contemporary cartographers. Could she have been inspired by the circular images of the medieval geographer Al-Idrisi? Many years later, looking at Sabine Rhétoré's sideways-on *Mare Nostrum* in Catania's Palazzo della Cultura (see page 116), I would be overcome with emotion at the memory of Evelyne. Throughout my childhood she had repeated a ritual that consisted of telling me to turn my back to the wall where the map was hanging, bend over until my chest touched my knees then describe what I could see with my head near the ground. If I burst out laughing she would reprimand me, 'If you think you're seeing the map the right way up now, you're wrong. There's no right way and no wrong way. There's just the way of showing us the world.'

*

As far back as I can remember I practised this technique of inversion. Quite soon I began to suggest others to her. At angles of 90 degrees. Even 45. Whenever I got the chance I would stand with my legs apart and bend over to shift my viewpoint of the street, cars, passers-by, my left, my right. Only the centre stayed in the centre. The swimming instructor, too. Even in him I would later seek traces of the blind alterity that led him to deny the otherness of his prey. I hadn't been the only one – I'd learn that later. At the time I made do with regularly dragging a chair over to my windowsill, climbing on to it and leaning out to see what

might happen to wounds if we looked at them topsy-turvy. Feeling the blood rush to my head and seeing a vision of fishing boats from below reassured me. Apparently all we had to do was upend the hourglass of our thoughts – and our pain – to imagine the sky in the place of the sea, and liners moving backwards. Evelyne approved. She was the first to pursue reality into a shameful corner. Like a cube whose every side must be measured, even at the risk of finding unexpected angles. She would take me by the hand and, with her limping gait, draw me to the window. The sound of twittering rose up from below: a family of birds had set up home in one of the railway carriages. She pointed to them.

'There was a time, you see, when war wasn't our only destiny. When a railway network was set up to link the port towns along our coast and the big cities of our neighbouring countries, which, in order to survive after the fall of the empires, unfortunately allowed themselves to be seduced by the trap of nationalism – a dirty thing. Then, one day, having grown used to defining ourselves through adversity, we sought enemies even in our closest neighbours. Until we reached the point of no return. There lies the Lebanese problem. Still, the railway you see here is the symbol of national union. Of our potential federation.'

To illustrate her point she opened a drawer of her dresser and took out an old map, so yellowed that it looked like parchment, that her father had left her. The paper, crinkled by humidity, set out the network of lines that had gradually been opened since 1895, at the time of the Beirut–Damas–Hauran Ottoman Railway Company. So the carriages hadn't always fulfilled the function of

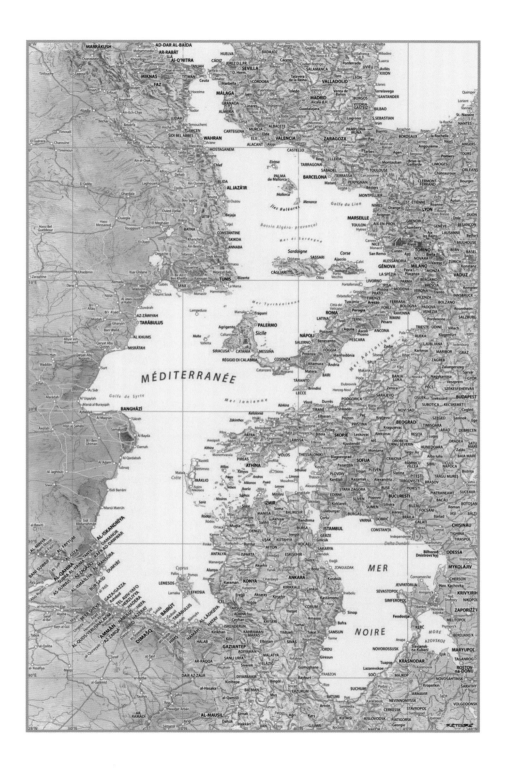

THE PASSENGER   Hyam Yared

> 'One day, having grown used to defining ourselves through adversity, we sought enemies even in our closest neighbours. Until we reached the point of no return. There lies the Lebanese problem.'

carcasses, and the project of linking Beirut to Damascus, the Beqaa Valley to Homs in Syria, Damascus to Jaffa, Homs to Tripoli on the northern coast of Lebanon and, further still, Beirut to Haifa via Saida (Sidon) wasn't simply a utopia. In fact, many people had followed the progress of the construction of this network under French rule and during the time of the young, independent Lebanese Republic after 1943. As the grey of her eyes intensified, Evelyne would stop breathing, either short of breath or from nostalgia – probably both. She would quickly fold up the map, as though she couldn't bear to remember.

*

My mother was not in agreement. She said her mother-in-law was raving. Fearing Evelyne's influence over me, she monitored our tête-à-têtes, perfecting the merciless art of interruption. Whenever she saw us side by side on Evelyne's balcony hanging under the Ottoman-inspired arcades of the family home built in the pure tradition of the early 20th century, my mother would find an excuse to bring me back down to earth. 'Your swimming lesson – you're going to miss it. Your piano lesson. Have

'Mediterranean Without Borders', a sideways-on map of the Mediterranean, drawn by Sabine Rhétoré and reproduced with the kind permission of the cartographer.

you finished your homework? What are you doing? Get a move on.'

Sometimes she would direct her anger at Evelyne. 'Will you stop putting absurd ideas about ancient interbreeding and imaginary upside-down worlds into my daughter's head? In wartime it's a crime against identity. There's only one way of fighting this, and that's by looking inwards. God helps those who help themselves – does that mean anything to you? Ever since the great plagues, only confinement has worked to contain pandemics. War is one of them. Your nostalgia for a country where Christians, Muslims, Druze, Shias, Sunnis and Jews lived in peace is way out of date, do you hear? Out of date. Don't rub history up the wrong way. Do I need to remind you how it was that your son and I left Aley, part of a Druze region and bastion of the birth of the Lebanon that you talk about with such wistfulness? Do I need to tell you again that without that phone call from Jalal – who was Druze, I admit – we would have suffered the same fate as our neighbours, murdered in their home after their phone line was cut? He called out of friendship. He saved us, it's true. But I have no illusions about it. Friendship aside, he didn't leave his region. He stayed there because he knows, and he's not wrong, that he can't come here any more than we would be welcome there. He wouldn't survive here. Our militia would make sure he understood that. And the whole neighbourhood.

And they'd be right. I've got the greatest respect for him, but the one piece of advice I'd give him would be that everyone should keep to their own home and the sheep will be watched over. Your multicultural Lebanon? A fantasy! Do you hear me? A fantasy. It's in the past!'

*

My parents' attitude of withdrawal didn't take shape straight away. It took root timidly. First, during those dinner parties when everyone offered up their opinion on the future of Lebanese Christians confined to districts that were majority Christian and on the need to avoid movement between communities that might destabilise the denominational separation that the war had naturally brought about. Almost a blessing in disguise, it would seem, for my parents, for whom accepting mixed marriages was like injecting yourself with a poison that had no antidote.

'Here,' my mother would say, 'we're Levantines and majority Christian.'

'Thank goodness!' my father would retort.

'God save us from invasions,' she would add. 'Our militia protects us from them. While the militia is here we've nothing to fear. The Muslims just have to behave themselves.'

These discussions generally turned sour faster than milk. My mother's mouth would fill with words as sharp as the whistle of sniper bullets in the centre of this divided town. A mainly Christian east; a Muslim west. When it was put that way my grandmother lamented, language would inevitably become a dividing line. At the age of twelve I didn't yet understand my luck in belonging to a country born of the sum of its minorities. My parents' vehemence prevented me from seeing it. Their friends, too, were fond of questioning our possible Arabness in favour of Phoenician origins extracted with forceps from a 'Phoenicianism' seized upon by far-right ideologies. If anybody was daring enough to insist on the Arabness of the east coast my mother would soon put them in their place.

'Arabness? What Arabness?'

'Ours, perhaps?' the unwise person might tentatively suggest.

'Ours? Are you mad? And this so-called Arabness isn't, you think, simply a fantasy created by the orientalism that everyone dislikes so much? Here we're Levantines, and before that we were Phoenicians, not Arabs. And, above all, Christians. This country was founded by the Maronites, and it will be protected by them. Only them.'

*

For a long time my Mediterranean was this crucible of reductive words where I believed life was summed up: a survival that justified any means. All words, including Phoenecianism, which, unlike my parents, Evelyne evoked to commemorate a time when the Phoenicians boasted of the Punic discovery of the West. At the very heart of this basin transformed into an umbilical cord constantly nourishing the north to the detriment of the south. She remembered fondly the time when the opposite was true, when the peoples of the eastern shores, fascinated by the other side of this basin, undertook the Punic colonisation of the west. As she gazed at the pine forest that ran down the flank of the hill she would ask me to tell her which European citizen would now remember that at the root of the word 'Europe' there was a Phoenician princess

New life grows amid the devastation resulting from the 2020 explosion in the Port of Beirut.

of that name, daughter of Agenor, carried off from a beach near Sidon by Zeus (who had taken the form of a bull) and brought to the Cretan hills at the gateway to the continent named after her. Just as there had been Dido, a Phoenician princess who had founded Carthage and left Tyre in search of Tunis.

'Ethnocentrism, my girl, hasn't always been a European thing. The story of the western side of the Mediterranean you see spread out before you was told by the Sumerians, the Phoenicians and the Egyptians in stories that allowed us to be trapped within orientalist concepts of "Arab" or "Levantine". Our big mistake was to allow ourselves to be limited by stories that we never fully shared. If we've been so disliked by certain people, it's because our story was badly told, and we've never forgiven ourselves for that.'

That was how I grew up, under the dual influence of contradictory stories with an imaginary world that was 'occupied' on the one hand by my parents and on the other by Evelyne's voice. We can never gauge the significance of those sidesteps that make us leave the herd, within which the mob reflex triumphs over the face of the other. Because a day always comes when the barricades shake, move and fall and with them the mental borders that alienate us. In Arabic the phrase for 'demarcation line' is *khoutout el tamess*. Translated literally, *tamess* means 'contact' or 'brushing against', so the phrase defining a fictitious line between two enemy forces is etymologically different in Arabic. This language defines something that separates in a way that doesn't omit the dimension of the link to the other, even if the other is an enemy. It is even said that when the end of the war was announced the soldiers on the two sides fell into each other's arms, showing that it doesn't really matter which side of the demarcation line we're on, the trenches are still the trenches, and peace still brings jubilation.

*

The day the demarcation line was abolished Evelyne died. I remember what time it was. Midnight. Her skin milky like a clear morning. I didn't cry. I looked out of her window. Lights filtered through the shutters of old houses competing here and there with neon-lit high-rises. That day the bay no longer called to me to leave. Its docks, backed up by the presence of the carriages, comforted me this time with the idea of staying. There was a challenge to take up: to investigate from within our fragmented memories. I felt charged with a mission to travel by car between all the stops along the coast the railway had been intended to link. Something drew me to this rusted metal. Like the proof that we hadn't dreamed the future in the light of a past that had never happened. That day the sparkling city exhorted me to show that it is possible to repair what pillage, nepotism and neglect had not spared. Almost to love their distortion. 'We don't abandon the dead who fell in battle,' Evelyne used to say. Rarely, in her eyes, had a country been so poorly protected from all the snares to which its location and its plurality left it exposed. I'd repeated it so often that I began to have a recurring dream. A huge crane in the middle of the Mediterranean was sinking enormous iron jaws into our coast in order to tear it away from the continent.

PHOENICIANISM

Of all the civilisations that grew up around the Mediterranean, the Phoenicians are perhaps the people most closely associated with the sea, which they crossed from end to end, founding colonies all the way to its far west. Settled in port cities along a narrow coastal strip that coincides with modern-day Lebanon and parts of Syria and Israel, they were expert sailors and shrewd traders. Many have tried to appropriate the legacy of the Phoenicians, starting with the Greeks and the Romans, but also the English under the Tudors as well as the Irish. So it comes as no surprise that after the First World War, under the French mandate in Syria and Lebanon, the Christian Maronites and the Druze, who were looking for a national identity, chose the ancient Phoenicians and their association with the Mediterranean to distinguish themselves from the neighbouring Arabs and Muslims, who were desert peoples, thus laying claim to thousands of years of historical continuity. Phoenicianism also dovetailed with the image of the Lebanese émigré, a modern Phoenician adventurer, heir to those skilled traders who sailed the sea. From a historical point of view there is no demonstrable link between the ancient Phoenicians and modern-day Lebanon, even less so since the very concept of the 'Phoenicians' has been called into question; the term is a Greek one, and more often than not it described Levantine traders in general rather than a specific people. The Phoenicians themselves, while sharing a language and religious practices, did not lay claim to a Phoenician identity but identified instead with their native cities, such as Tyre or Sidon – a disunited people who actually are fitting ancestors for the ravaged country that claims descent from them.

I would wake up drenched in sweat, almost disappointed to find everything still in the same place and attached to its conflict zone. I wanted it to be an island, surrounded by sea, with no direct neighbours. I'd mentioned this to my grandmother, who had barely reacted.

'The challenge is to reconnect with our alterities. And you? What are you doing? You dream of detaching yourself from it all. Let me tell you something. There isn't any real adversity. There's just the sort that we need to blame on scapegoats.'

At that precise moment I wondered which was a scapegoat: the swimming instructor or his prey. And a scapegoat for what? For what pain? What adversity? For a long time I tried to decipher her legacy. I'm still trying today. I'm sure that turning my pen against my own certitudes made me a writer. Like her map of the world. I didn't imagine then that in reconnecting with my coast I would, in my own turn, dismantle the toxic ties that link prey and predator in mutual hatred. Like two extremes seemingly entirely separate. The two sides of a suffering that Evelyne saw as twins. Like those of the Mediterranean Basin, which she said carried within it the pain of a mother wounded by her children mired in rivalry because neither of them has really had the courage to see in the other the reflection of their own face.

*

The carriages obsessed me for a long time before I put my plan into action. I looked at them from my window. I closed my eyes to immerse myself in the experience of a pile of rusted metal – what it would say if it could talk, as though I needed to identify with the carriages' abandonment. Nineteen years

later I would realise that I hadn't been so crazy: in 2019 this country staged one of its most spectacular demonstrations against neglect, corruption and mismanagement by its governing class. A feeling of collective abandonment united us. On 27 October 2019, on the eleventh day of a popular uprising set off by the dissident resurgence on 17 October, a human chain formed of tens of thousands of Lebanese people took shape along the east coast, people standing side by side for 170 kilometres, stretching from north to south in a gesture of unity, all faiths mixed together. The number of people involved was estimated at more than a hundred thousand, united in their will to send a clear message to those who were treating them as pawns in their predatory agenda of profit and gain. That day the carriages were represented by those tens of thousands of human beings side by side. We had simply needed to align our hearts and minds to restore a soul to these places. A will. A desire to live together. Nineteen years earlier I had also believed that it was not a vain endeavour to travel along the coast. I already saw myself as a mechanic repairing our fractured memories. At that time the north interested me less than the West, so vilified by my parents. I had to go there, and check that it's absurd to live with a compass that never points west.

I'd wanted to start from the abandoned station of Mar Mikhaël, located in a neighbourhood adjacent to what had been the Green Line. The hands standing still on the station clock gave this place, a symbol of the failure of our railway system, a feeling of decline. A sense that a train might turn up at any moment. As in the days when it did pass, no matter what. Irregular, carrying on despite the

Above: Ramlet al-Baida, Beirut's last public beach, deserted.
Opposite below: A boy watches an aeroplane take off from Beirut airport.

tion caused by war, it was delivering a message. Articulating what? Not peace in the strict sense. Perhaps a dialogue, albeit one performed by a train running for reasons of the commerce of combat. That train – I didn't know it at the time – represented suffering in need of a remedy, like the suffering endured by this country. And we were blind. Incapable of understanding the symbolic weight travelling along these rails.

*

war. I remember seeing the walls trembling. Windowpanes vibrating. A dull roar preceded it. Then it appeared, as if from nowhere. Surreal, with its chain of wagons loaded with food, merchandise and, perhaps, weapons. This train continued to run until 1996 with no regular timetable, providing impromptu transfers between one region and another, as though, despite all the dysfunc-

It was this weight that I wanted to take on. Without reservation. From east to west. On my route to the south, site of so many occupations – the fedayeen in Tsahal, the South Lebanon Army now replaced by Hezbollah – I followed the tracks from the station. Sometimes covered in cement or asphalt, sometimes

THE PASSENGER   Hyam Yared

city of Sidon, ancestor of Saida, built at the same time as its northern twin, Byblos, both bearing the marks of their various heritages: Babylonian, Roman and the legacy of the Crusades. Sand covered the track a few metres from the beach. A little further on was the sea. The railway track plunged into it almost like a suicide. It was the year 2000, and the country was jubilant at the prospect of reconstruction. I had got caught up in it, too, intoxicated by the idea of a country that might be reunited. Perhaps even rebuilt.

After Saida I arrived in Tyre, always held up by my parents as a rival to Byblos. Byblos this, Byblos that. They endowed this port, in the heart of the Christian area, with the status of a capital to which humanity, in their eyes, owed its greatest achievements: the alphabet and the

in grass and moss. More than once the rails ran into dead ends, so I had to continue on foot. I remember the ends of rails being like the ends of countries. It was that way in the ancient Phoenician

CYPRUS: WHERE STAR-CROSSED LOVERS TAKE THEIR FLIGHT

When a Middle Eastern marriage is deemed unacceptable there is always a last resort: take a flight to Cyprus and perhaps even tack on a couple of days' holiday. The island has become a destination for forbidden couples, far from the eyes of the imams, rabbis or priests as well as overly interfering parents, particularly for Lebanese and Israelis. In neither country is there any legal secular marriage, even less inter-religious or same-sex unions, but marriages that take place abroad are recognised. The Cypriot wedding business caters to ten thousand couples a year and so makes a reasonable contribution to the economy of an island that has always depended on tourism, in spite of its division and the political tensions between Greece and Turkey, which have led, among other things, to the abandonment of the resort of Varosha, Europe's most incredible ghost town. The place once regarded as the Cypriot answer to Saint-Tropez was occupied by the Turkish army in 1974, Greek citizens were forced to flee and the town's difficult position right by the Green Line and the buffer zone that cuts Cyprus in two led to it being completely abandoned, a case study to evaluate the effects of the disappearance of the human population on an urban environment. In recent years, however, things have started to change. The Turkish Republic of Northern Cyprus (with the support of President Erdoğan of Turkey) is working to gradually open up some parts of Varosha, leading to protests from Greek Cypriots and the international community.

extraction of the purple dye that boosted the popularity of Phoenician textiles among colonial networks and traders all along the coast. Byblos, as magnified through the lens of identity by my parents, was just one link in the chain. When I discovered Tyre and its hippodrome that seems to float over the sea, I don't know what it was that took my breath away, whether a sense of wonder or an aesthetic shock like that experienced by Stendhal on coming out of Santa Croce. 'Life,' he wrote, 'drained away' within him, and he walked 'fearing to fall'. I didn't fall. I stayed upright. An overload of culture caught me in its grasp. Of sheer beauty charged with a distillation of diverse civilisations. Someone once told me that linear time doesn't exist. Researchers and scientists even agree that all it takes to conceive of the verticality of time is to imagine a dimension in which, at a precise geographical point, it would be possible to overlay Phoenician shops, Alexander the Great's troops and Ottoman janissaries sitting in the lotus position on tanks belonging to the Syrian, Lebanese, Israeli or even UN armies. Where did the rails come into all this? A sort of linear incarnation of compressed time. That day I felt as though something shot through me, something I couldn't understand. I found it hard to breathe. Surrounded by colonnades ten metres tall, I almost felt I could glimpse the waving hair of Princess Dido, as she embarked for Carthage on a boat of the Phoenician fleet. Haifa wasn't far away. A century earlier I would have been able to join her, riding a donkey or in a cart, but barbed wire separated us now. All these obstructed routes filled me with profound bitterness. The face of my Mediterranean no longer resembled the one I saw reflected in Evelyne's eyes when she

'To conceive of the verticality of time is to imagine a dimension in which, at a precise geographical point, it would be possible to overlay Phoenician shops, Alexander the Great's troops and Ottoman janissaries sitting in the lotus position on tanks belonging to the Syrian, Lebanese, Israeli or even UN armies.'

gazed out at the water, in times of peace or increasing violence, as though seeking answers to the question of our shattered alterities.

*

My own Mediterranean has nothing to do with the one that those who preferred conflict to dialogue, borders to free exchange, greed to the preservation of intangible legacies hoped to bequeath to us. Mine is elsewhere. To paraphrase the words of Antoine de Saint-Exupéry in *The Little Prince*, 'it's the time we've spent' for the Mediterranean that makes my Mediterranean so important, so unique in our eyes. The geographical location matters little. It's linking places to their memories that counts, seeking the blindest spots in the black holes of our recall, the continuity of a future anchored in a consensual past. My own Mediterranean has the face of a people that has been called aggressive and incompetent when it comes to its own destiny. However, nobody else has done so much to cling to its diversity and be its wounded ambassador, even of civil war. Because what is a war if not the occasional failure of a desire to live together? What is peace if not the refusal of a society to allow itself to be engulfed by the kind of ethnic hatred to which some would like it to succumb so that

they might profit from the situation? The bonfires are ready, and the country's unprecedented economic crisis is the ideal tinderbox for a new conflict. And yet this society remains and persists, heroic in its will not to give in to armed conflict to settle its internal discord. It thereby proves its rootedness in the fundamental conviviality of its identity but also the humanity of its inevitable shifting population. I want, here, to grasp the idea that beyond our differences from one side to the other of the same Mediterranean Basin the opposing fluxes of this coastline can have the effect of a centrifuge for our thoughts and our imaginations. Through Evelyne's voice I have learned to turn everything on its head, to mix things up, to re-examine our certitudes, to look from new angles armed with a 360-degree compass that is no longer weighted on the inside. Only then can we hope for increased closeness between the different sides, themselves hostages of a fascination increased by the confrontation between these worlds. Sometimes, in memory of Evelyne, I still bend over to see my life upside down. Upended. From the outside. Unadorned. With borders tested by our shifting compasses. Our pains. Our languages. Our memories. It's there, my Mediterranean. It's not dying in vain. It's handing down. 🖋

The Irascible, the Hot, the Cold and the Mad: The Ill-Tempered Winds of the Mediterranean

Here we meet four winds – the bora, sirocco, mistral and meltemi – which, with their forceful personalities, have shaped habits, customs, agriculture, myth and architecture along the coasts of the Mediterranean.

NICK HUNT
Photography by Rachel Cobb

A wind-bent olive tree, Beaumes-de-Venise, Provence, shaped by decades of exposure to the mistral.

B efore me lies a maritime map of the Mediterranean Sea. The predominant currents are shown as arrows flowing in an anticlockwise loop, eastwards along the North African coast and back towards the Atlantic again, navigating the complicated coastline of southern Europe. Looking closer I can see that this grand circulation is muddled by two smaller gyres in the Ionian and Levantine seas and by innumerable local interactions as the water encounters peninsulas, islands, inlets and other obstacles, producing a dizzying mass of arrows that spiral in all directions.

But above the Mediterranean there is another sea: a churning, heaving ocean of gas rather than of liquid. Just as the visible sea below is shaped by the way the water interacts with the land that presses it on all sides, so the invisible sea above is a product of chaotically clashing factors: low pressure over the Atlantic; high pressure over the Sahara; rivers of air pouring through passes in mountains from the High Atlas to the Alps; cold fronts and warm fronts periodically advancing and retreating; and the atmospheric upheaval between oceanic and continental climates. Like the map of currents, the map of winds is a psychedelic panorama of arrows twisting, bending and flowing from north to south and south to north in a chaos of fluid dynamics.

It is a map of this second sea that makes me fall in love with wind – and, specifically, the named winds of the Mediterranean. These great aeolian powers blow at particular times of year down atmospheric corridors they have followed for millennia and have profound – and often surprising – effects on landscape, ecology, agriculture, commerce, shipping, industry, tourism, gastronomy, architecture, history, religion and psychology. They are both cursed and celebrated, greeted with elation and fear, loved and hated in equal measure – and sometimes all these things at the same time.

Most people are familiar with everyday, 'directional' winds: northerlies, which blow from the north; southeasterlies, which blow from the southeast. Their names, prosaic and matter-of-fact, simply derive from the compass directions from which they blow. But the winds I am interested in speak in poetry, not prose. The fact that they are endowed with names suggests that they have personalities, and certainly they often seem like larger-than-life characters whose mood swings, whims and tempestuous rages have shaped culture throughout history – and continue to shape it today.

I have been lucky, and unlucky, enough to meet four of these characters and will introduce each in turn. Meet the meltemi, the sirocco, the bora and the mistral.

NICK HUNT is the author of three travel books, including *Where the Wild Winds Are: Walking Europe's Winds from the Pennines to Provence,* a finalist for the Edward Stanford Travel Writing Award. He also works as an editor and co-director of the Dark Mountain Project. His latest book is *Red Smoking Mirror,* an alternate-history novel. nickhuntscrutiny.com

RACHEL COBB is a photographer based in New York City whose work focuses on social issues, the natural world and current affairs. Her photographs have been published in international magazines, newspapers and books, and her work has been awarded many prizes. She has exhibited in solo and group exhibitions both in the USA and in France. Her critically acclaimed monograph *Mistral: The Legendary Wind of Provence* (Damiani, 2018) is dedicated to one of the four winds profiled in this article.

A coastal storm on Prado Beach, Marseilles; the waves whipped up by the mistral can reach as high as nine metres.

MELTEMI: THE BAD-TEMPERED ONE

We have been on the island for a day when the wind starts blowing. It comes from the north, cold and dry, driving white horses over the sea, and it doesn't let up for a week. The ferries are all cancelled. My friend and I – aged eighteen, island-hopping around the Cyclades – are sleep-ing on the beach, and planned to stay for a couple of nights on tiny Koufonisia before heading to one of the larger islands. But the wind has stranded us here. It just keeps on blowing. It whistles over the low stone wall we have built in an attempt to shelter ourselves, covering our belongings in sand, and keeps us awake long into the night with its moans and howls.

Having grown up in rainy Britain, the thing that feels most alien to me is the combination of gale-force wind with the clear blue skies and dazzling sunshine that greets us every morning. In fact, the more violently it blows, the lovelier the weather is. It makes me feel slightly mad, as if the

> 'The meltemi is a reminder that nothing is "local" in the world of weather, that climates are intimately connected, that nowhere is separate from anywhere else.'

wind is tormenting us. I start talking to it, begging it to go away, to release my friend and I from this surreal captivity and let us escape to Athens again, where our homeward flight is waiting.

And then, after five days, it stops. We catch the next morning's ferry. It isn't until we reach the mainland, sleep-deprived and weather-scoured, that I learn that the wind has a name. It is called meltemi.

Some say this name derives from the Italian *mal tempo*, 'bad weather', but the theory I prefer gives it a Turkish origin translating as 'bad tempered'. The meltemi blows mostly in the summer, reaching the peak of its moodiness in July and August – although sometimes it still howls through September and into October – and can reach gale-force strength, up to eight on the Beaufort scale.

The meltemi always comes from the north, billowing into the Aegean Sea and the eastern Mediterranean from the mountainous bulk of the Balkans,

Tourists buffeted by gusts from the mistral on the Pont Saint-Bénézet, also known as the Pont d'Avignon.

THE PASSENGER   Nick Hunt

squeezed between the opposing land masses of Greece and Anatolia. As it reaches the sea it encounters islands – like the one on which my eighteen-year-old self was temporarily stranded – which channel its currents this way and that, increasing its speed and making its effects less predictable. The Cyclades bear the brunt of its wrath, especially Naxos, Andros and Tinos, and the party island of Mykonos is often said to be the windiest of all – proof that freezing, gale-force winds do no harm to tourism. In fact, its chill is welcomed for reducing scorching temperatures; without this effect the Aegean islands might be too hot to visit in summer.

Landlubbing tourists might welcome the wind, but sensible seafarers certainly don't; a powerful meltemi can be perilous for sailors, arriving in clear weather and blowing up without warning. As I experienced on Koufonisia, the blue skies and sunshine do not change, there are no dark clouds or thunderstorms, but suddenly the air is moving at 60 km/h. In a matter of minutes the sea can transform from a gentle swell into four-metre-high waves, dashing moored boats against the quays and scattering ships across the sea; experienced sailors will head for harbour or anchor in the lee of an island to wait for the fury to abate. Sometimes this can take days.

There is another, more ancient name for this bad-tempered wind: the Etesian wind, from the Greek *etesios*, meaning 'annual'. It has been a dependable presence since at least the 3rd century BCE, when Philip II of Macedon – father of Alexander the Great – used it as an aeolian force field to prevent hostile Persian fleets from pursuing him home in the summer. For thousands of

HEADWINDS

Winds with a strong personality are also, almost by definition, capricious and irregular. This is one of the reasons, aside from the technical difficulties of dealing with frequently deep water, for the slower speed of commercial development of offshore sources of renewable energy in the Mediterranean by comparison with areas such as the North Sea. On dry land there are plenty of turbines. Spain was once the European leader and is still one of the countries with the highest installed capacity, but the sector never entirely recovered from the 2008 financial crisis. Obviously, the countries making the running are those without abundant reserves of gas and oil. Turkey has erected turbines all along the Aegean coast – which produce 10 per cent of its electricity (the average in the EU, which began a lot earlier, is 15 per cent) – and Morocco has unveiled an ambitious investment programme with the aim of deriving half of its energy from renewable sources by 2030. But, in terms of offshore wind, the Mediterranean's potential has yet to be exploited. The first wind farm at sea was only opened in 2022, off the coast of Taranto, Italy, an investment of €80 million that produces energy equivalent to the annual usage of sixty thousand people. France is close behind, with three floating wind farms in the Gulf of Lion, and many other projects have already been approved, a welcome contribution to the EU objective of generating 42.5 per cent of electricity from renewable sources by 2030.

years the Etesian/meltemi has determined life and fate across the eastern Mediterranean, but its meteorological origins lie much further afield: this local Greek wind can trace its roots to annual depressions over South Asia and the summer monsoon of the Indian subcontinent. The iconic windmills of Mykonos and Santorini, the quintessential postcard image of Greece, ultimately owe their existence to rainclouds over Kolkata and Delhi. The meltemi is a reminder that nothing is 'local' in the world of weather, that climates are intimately connected, that nowhere is separate from anywhere else.

And leaving the Greek islands behind, no wind better illustrates the connections between distant continents than the many-named wind that blows from the other direction.

SIROCCO: THE AFRICAN WIND

Halfway up a Slovenian mountain I turn back to admire the view and see only a grubby blanket. To the south the land and sea have been covered in a pall, a pinkish-greyish haze that masks and muddies everything. From this altitude I can see that the sky has been cut in two, divided into neat halves: clarity in the north and darkness in the south, opposing weather fronts clashing like armies over the Adriatic.

The sight takes my breath away, in more ways than one. During the next couple of days the murk advances from the coast, stifling the atmosphere and pressing uncomfortably on my lungs. In some regions cars on the street are covered in a layer of sediment – I am told it is red sand from the Sahara carried over the Mediterranean, a phenomenon that was historically known as 'blood rain'. Despite the unhealthy conditions it feels miraculous to me that this spot on the Balkan coast is connected by a current of air to the sweltering deserts of Africa.

Again, I learn that the wind has a name. Locally it is nicknamed the jugo, from the Slavic word for 'south', but it also goes by the ghibli and the xaloc. In most of the Mediterranean, though, it is simply the sirocco.

In a region swept by dry northerlies – rivers of cold continental air squeezed through the Alps and the Balkan mountains – the sirocco is the foetid breath of the sweltering south. Connecting North Africa and southern Europe, it is a wind of contradictions: a dust-dry desert wind that brings damp and humidity. On its long journey from the Sahara it picks up volumes of sand, and when it reaches the rolling waves it becomes swollen with moisture – combining the desert and the sea, it erupts on to Europe's coastline. Its multivarious local names are an indicator of its range, affecting the climates of Spain, Portugal, France, Italy, Corsica, Sardinia, Sicily, Malta, the Balkans, Greece, Turkey and the Levant. In Venice, combined with an exceptional tide, the sirocco is a contributing factor to the *acqua alta* phenomenon, exacerbating the drowning of one of Europe's most treasured cities.

Most commonly blowing in autumn and spring, this so-called 'African wind' can reach up to 100 km/h, disrupting shipping the length and breadth of the Mediterranean. Because of its humidity it is associated with less-than-salubrious health effects, including lethargy, breathlessness, insomnia, headaches, irritability, anxiety and even asthma attacks. This might sound like superstition – 'an ill wind that blows nobody any good' – but science suggests that certain winds have deleterious

In the famous definition coined by Predrag Matvejević, the Mediterranean is 'the sea of closeness' and the Adriatic 'the sea of intimacy'. The Adriatic is small, a little under 139,000 square kilometres, with an average width of no more than 150 kilometres. It lacks natural ports on the Italian side, while the eastern shore is labyrinthine. Generally narrow and dangerous, it is subject to unpredictable weather because of the mountain ranges that surround it and from which vigorous winds such as the bora descend. While the Mediterranean sits in a basin, the description is even more apt for the Adriatic: a semi-closed basin joined to the rest of the Mediterranean to the south, where it narrows to form the Strait of Otranto, the boundary between the Adriatic and Ionian seas. Fernand Braudel described it as a 'narrow sea where the Mediterranean divides'. In fact, the Adriatic replicates the essential traits of the Mediterranean: the limited and defined area of the maritime space, making it a familiar, homely place defined by close proximity. On clear days from Monte Conero in Italy you can see the mountains of Dalmatia; in a hydrofoil you can cross it in a few hours. And the Adriatic literally places several different worlds opposite one another. What was once known as the Gulf of Venice has a glorious past, and it marked the boundary between the Roman and Greek worlds, then between the Latin and Slavic worlds and finally between Christians and Muslims. It is 'the Mediterranean of the Mediterranean' wrote the historian Egidio Ivetic in *The History of the Adriatic*, summing up its characteristics, adding that to think about the Adriatic is to think about the most profound history of the Mediterranean and of Europe.

effects on physiology and psychology, ranging from bodily stress reactions to fluctuating serotonin levels. Certainly, the people I met in Slovenia and Croatia during the week-long sirocco that started blowing as I climbed that mountain were in little doubt that the southerly wind made them sick.

Perhaps the most vivid illustration of the sirocco's baleful aspect is that phenomenon of blood rain – red sand from North African deserts periodically dumped over Europe, sometimes as far north as Scotland and Norway – which has appalled and horrified communities throughout history. Understandably, this ghoulish occurrence was seen as a portent of disaster, announcing everything from Viking invasion to the untimely death of kings; when blood rain fell over Paris in the year 582, Gregory of Tours wrote that people were 'so stained and spotted that they stripped themselves of their clothing in horror'.

Sailors fear the sirocco not for its sanguine side effects but for the simpler, deadlier reason that it can capsize ships.

The Irascible, the Hot, the Cold and the Mad

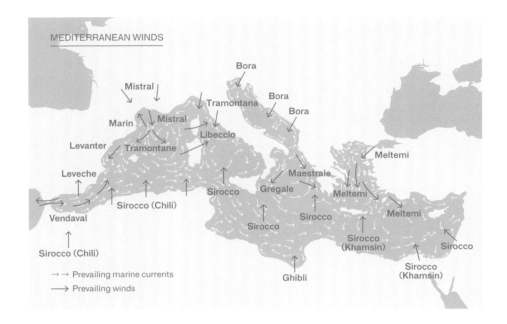

MEDITERRANEAN WINDS

Bora
Mistral
Tramontana
Bora
Bora
Marin
Mistral
Libeccio
Levanter
Tramontane
Leveche
Meltemi
Sirocco
Maestrale
Gregale
Meltemi
Meltemi
Sirocco (Chili)
Vendaval
Sirocco
Meltemi
Sirocco
Sirocco (Chili)
Sirocco
Sirocco
(Khamsin)
Ghibli
Sirocco
(Khamsin)

→ → Prevailing marine currents
⟶ Prevailing winds

But after that barrage of negative press it is important to note that the southerly wind has significant positives. Without its regular warming breath the climate of much of southern Europe would be less conducive to olives and grapes, which have been cultivated in the region for around seven thousand years; and Adriatic fishermen would go without their anchovies, which can only be caught in the warmer seas brought about by sirocco conditions. A vision of Mediterranean cooking without anchovies, olives or wine hints at how this Saharan wind shapes European identity – a force that is not bad or good but part of the complex tapestry of meteorological factors that make the Mediterranean – and its cultures – what it is.

Winds often work in opposites: against this hot, wet southerly blows another cold, dry northerly. And to encounter this one is to meet an ancient god.

BORA: THE GOD OF WINTER

I am in the city of Split, on the Croatian coast, when I hear the call 'Crna bura! Black bora!' The woman who owns the guesthouse I'm staying in is shouting in the street, gesturing towards the sky, which has turned ominously dark. Within minutes freezing rain is pouring horizontally, and I am almost knocked flat when I venture into the street, forced to shield my face from debris whizzing past like shrapnel.

Within the hour the black bora – characterised by dark skies and rain – has swept the moisture from the sky and transformed into the white bora, clean and dry rather than wet, but every bit as violent. The sun is bright and the sky is blue, but the temperature has plummeted, and the northeast-facing side of every object in sight has been covered in a crystalline layer of ice. The air is so cold it hurts, and the wind so strong it frightens me. From the quayside, white-capped waves are being driven furiously offshore – the bora blows from inland, through passes in the Dinaric Alps – and I hope that any sailors have heeded the words of the local saying: 'When bora sails, you don't.'

The Adriatic – that long, skinny inlet of the Mediterranean that separates Italy from the Balkans and the Latin from the Slavic worlds – is the natural playground of the bora, which rages from Trieste in the north as far south as Montenegro. It occurs when dry, frigid air builds up on the continental side of the Dinaric Alps that run parallel to the coast; as the atmospheric pressure equalises, this air is sucked, with enormous violence, through a number of mountain passes (locally known as 'mouths') into the warmer, lower-pressure area over the sea.

The bora can often reach hurricane strength, and every year it inflicts tremendous damage on the coast, leaving a trail of destruction that includes trees ripped up by their roots, roofs torn off houses, capsized ships, trucks overturned on motorways and bridges and other infrastructure destroyed. A powerful bora can fell tens of thousands of trees on the Karst – the exposed limestone plateau shared between Italy and Slovenia – and in summer 2022 it combined with record-breaking temperatures to spread devastating wildfires, burning 350,000 hectares of forest. Conversely, in February 2012 – during the European cold wave, which saw temperatures in the Balkans plummet to minus 15 degrees Celsius – the bora had the opposite effect, creating fantastical wind-formed ice sculptures up and down the coast. In that same year, on the island of Pag, in truly apocalyptic scenes, thousands of fish were blown out of the sea to litter the frozen shoreline.

It should not be surprising that such awesome power was once worshipped as a god. Depicted on the Tower of the Winds – an ancient marble *horologion* at the base of the Acropolis in Athens – are the eight wind deities known as the Anemoi. Each is winged, with a billowing cloak, facing his respective compass point, and chief among them is Boreas, the god of the north: scowling, with ice in his beard, bearing a conch shell that represents the howling of his voice. Unlike Zephyrus to the west – bringer of spring, holding fruits and flowers – Boreas is the harbinger of winter and destruction. This ominous character is where the bora gets its name from.

But Boreas was two-faced, linked with life as well as death. In the form of a raging stallion he would fertilise horses in spring – it was believed that a mare would fall pregnant if placed rump-first to the north – and, just like the Etesian wind, he was a force for protection, too: responsible for wrecking an invading Persian fleet in 480 BCE. Centuries later the bora is said to have changed the course of history again. In 394 CE, in the Vipava Valley in what is now Slovenia, two armies battled for the future of the Roman Empire: the Christian Emperor Theodosius I and his pagan challenger Eugenius. During the Battle of the Frigid River (also known as the Battle of the Bora), legend says that a powerful northerly blew the arrows of Eugenius' troops back into his own ranks, causing panicked retreat. The Christian army won the day, and the new religion went on to spread rapidly throughout Europe.

Whatever the truth, or untruth, of that tale, the bora's influence on its surroundings can be seen everywhere. A common clue to its presence is the crazy angle of the trees: in wind-prone

'Medicane' might sound like a mobility aid, but it is actually a portmanteau of 'Mediterranean hurricane', a weather phenomenon that is growing ever more frequent. These Mediterranean cyclones are on a smaller scale than their tropical counterparts but share similar mechanisms. They were once seen as mainly autumnal events, forming when the first waves of cold, dry air pass over the still relatively warm surface of the Mediterranean close to its annual temperature peak after months of exposure to the summer sun. Their intensification seems to be linked to climate change; from the end of the Second World War to the present day around a hundred have been recorded, but the most violent have been those that have occurred since 2017, which have mainly hit Greece and southern Italy. The extreme heat of the summer of 2022 was followed by anomalous medicanes in the middle of winter and even in early March. Mediterranean cyclones are accompanied by intense rain, stormy gusts of wind and waves of up to seven metres. They are smaller than tropical cyclones both in terms of average size (a diameter of between two hundred and four hundred kilometres) and duration (between one and two days), but they share the same classic eye, a central, cloudless zone, in which the temperature can be as much as 8 degrees Celsius above the surrounding cold air. And while we are on the subject of global warming and its unpleasant effects, another consequence is the proliferation of jellyfish in the Mediterranean, also helped by years of overfishing that has decimated their predators.

regions cypresses and pines are bent at 45-degree angles, permanently shaped and stunted by the prevailing gusts. Across the Slovenian Karst, farmhouses are built like fortresses, and villages on the Croatian coast are constructed like labyrinths to deflect or 'baffle' the wind as it hurtles through the streets. In the Italian city of Trieste, specially designed 'bora ropes' are slung along roads and intersections for people to cling to during high winds, and the roofs of houses are often adorned with heavy rocks – known locally as 'little doves' – to stop their tiles being ripped away when the bora blows. Trieste even has the Bora Museum full of wind-related artefacts, including a display of 'bottled winds' sent from all around the world.

Like the sirocco, the bora leaves a distinctive mark on gastronomy. In winter, when the wind is at its coldest, Karst peasants would traditionally hang their hams in an open window, allowing the frigid air to cure the meat naturally. This technique is still followed to produce the delicious prosciutto (*pršut* in Slovenian) for which carloads of Italian foodies arrive in the spring and summer; the cold wind is also essential for the production of wine from Teran grapes, requiring no pesticides. Further south, Croatian island sheep's cheese has a distinctive saline taste, as the grass on which the animals graze has been salted by the wind.

Now grapes and cheese lead us to France for an encounter with one last wind – perhaps the most famous, or infamous, in the Mediterranean.

MISTRAL: THE WIND OF MADNESS

I meet my fourth and final wind on the banks of the River Rhône. I am walking south towards the sea, past vineyards,

The 'Windy Mountain', Mont Ventoux,
lives up to its name.

a malicious, nagging presence that I cannot seem to escape, howling and whistling, relentless in its intensity. As with the meltemi years ago, I beg my tormentor to leave me alone even as my eye is struck by the dazzling clarity it brings.

When it finally stops I have glimpsed its two faces: beauty and madness.

pylons and lavender fields, when I feel a powerful hand pushing at my back. At first it is like a helpful friend, then an insistent personal trainer; soon I am flying along the path, stumbling with the speed.

The sky, which has been overcast, clears, and a pure blue corridor opens up above the Rhône, a sunlit pathway pointing south; most striking of all is the magical clarity of the golden light. The rooftops and steeples of distant villages are suddenly brought into perfect focus, and I can see for miles. But my ears ring with the cold.

I am following the Chemin de Saint-Jacques, an ancient pilgrims' path, and for days the wind steers me south – a truly miraculous presence. It is only after the third day that it starts to turn diabolical,

Taking its name from the Latin *magistralis*, which means 'masterly', the mistral plunges towards the Mediterranean's heart like an arrow. Rising around the town of Valence – where the south of France begins – it blows due south down the natural corridor of the Rhône Valley, which channels and intensifies the force of the wind as it narrows, past the medieval walls of Avignon and the café-bars of Arles, through the wetlands of the Camargue and into the Gulf of Lion. Once at sea it wreaks havoc on shipping, in extreme conditions reaching up to 180 km/h and producing

The Irascible, the Hot, the Cold and the Mad

> 'By sweeping moisture and pollution from the air, the mistral creates the clarity and dazzling luminosity that – along with easy living, balmy temperatures and cheap wine – drew generations of artists to live and work in the south of France.'

seven-metre-high waves; experienced sailors know to watch for dark lenticular clouds at sunset, which are said to provide advance warning of an approaching blast. Another intensely dry, frigid wind, the mistral is sometimes nicknamed *mange-fange*, 'mud-eater', for its desiccating effects. An old saying goes that it is strong enough to blow the tail off a donkey.

Many people know the mistral from the Tour de France cycling race, the route of which leads up Mont Ventoux – 'Windy Mountain' – the highest point in Provence. Wind speeds at its summit can reach hurricane strength, knocking competitors off their bikes and causing the race to be rerouted. In the summer, regular cyclists know to plan their tours southwards, not northwards, for fear of meeting the mistral en route – mirroring the migration of birds to the Bouches-du-Rhône wetlands and beyond.

As with the bora, clues in the landscape announce when you're in mistral territory – all you need to look for are windowless northern walls. Traditional *mas* farmhouses are built with blank walls facing north to shield their inhabitants from the mistral, with windows, gardens and family life sheltered in the building's lee. This follows an ancient pattern: at an archaeological site near Nice excavations have revealed 400,000-year-old fire pits surrounded by the butchered bones of aurochs, rhinoceroses and elephants, constructed – just like those farmhouses – with high walls to the north. A truly ancient presence here, the mistral has been blowing in these lands for a long time.

Another clue can be seen in church steeples with iron gantries in place of bell towers, allowing the northerly wind to whistle through unimpeded. Or in the traditional *santons* of local Nativity scenes, figurines representing stock characters from Provençal life, one of which depicts an old man holding down his hat to prevent the mistral from blowing it away. But perhaps the most striking landscape feature is the rows of cypresses planted along an east–west axis – across the wind's path – which act as living windbreaks to shelter the vineyards and orchards behind.

The mistral's greatest gift to Provence – and to the history of Western art – is surely the clear golden light for which the region is famed. By sweeping moisture and pollution from the air, the wind creates the clarity and dazzling luminosity that – along with easy living, balmy temperatures and cheap wine – drew generations of artists to live and work in the south of France. Pablo Picasso, Marc Chagall, Paul Cézanne, Paul Gauguin, Claude Monet and Henri Matisse all set up their easels here, but no painter was more associated with the wind than Vincent Van Gogh.

After moving to Arles in Provence in 1888, Van Gogh painted some of his greatest works there, attracted by the light produced by the mistral. The disturbing effect of the wind is ever present in his canvases, where nothing is ever still – every brushstroke twists and coils with furious energy. But at the same time as inspiring his art, the mistral provided a soundtrack to his increasing depression and madness; his letters frequently complain about being tormented by the wind that can rage for weeks on end, never letting him rest. In two short years of mistral exposure Van Gogh painted more than two hundred canvases, but the intensity proved too much: after cutting off his ear and spending time in an asylum, he tragically took his own life in 1890.

Perhaps it should come as no surprise that the mistral has another name: it is commonly known as 'the wind of madness' (and in the Occitan tongue it is called *le vent du fada*, or 'the idiot wind'). Superstitiously thought to blow for three, six or nine days, it produces an incessant howling that is said to drive people crazy, and every year this tormenting presence is blamed for depression, insomnia, irrational behaviour, anxiety and even murders and suicides. Historically, the wind of madness was considered a mitigating factor in cases of *crimes passionnels*: if you could prove that the mistral made you do it, a sympathetic Provençal judge might reduce your sentence.

*

There are many more named Mediterranean winds – from the Levanter of Gibral-

tar to the khamsin of the Holy Land, from the gregale of Malta to the leveche of Spain – each with its personality and its good and evil aspects. But the meltemi of the Aegean, the sirocco of North Africa, the bora of the Adriatic and the mistral of Provence are a world of weather in themselves, full of beauty, madness, joy, destruction and contradictions. I have been privileged to meet them all and look forward to (and slightly dread) feeling their powerful breath again.

As they say in Italy: *buon vento*, 'good wind'! ✒

RED GOLD

ROCÍO PUNTAS BERNET
Translated by Stephen Smithson
Photography by Laura León Gómez

A tuna is hooked during the *ronqueo*
(butchering, one of the stages of the
almadraba) at the port of Barbate, Cadiz.

Tuna fishing in the Strait of Gibraltar dates back at least as far as the time of the Phoenicians, but in recent decades, following the explosion in the popularity of sushi, fishing for bluefin tuna has expanded to a previously unimaginable level and led to new forms of fish farming to feed the insatiable demand.

141

'Your entry into the world's cuisine was your death sentence.

I would never have thought such gastronomic success possible. When I was a young child, to me you were just great, stinking creatures. Of the year's catch only two specimens used to end up in the hands of the villagers. One would be sacrificed to the Virgen de la Luz, Our Lady of Light, the other divided up among the *almadrabre-ros,* the tuna fishermen. No one counted your true worth in those days, that you are the largest and most valuable of all tuna, the *Thunnus thynnus*, the red tuna or Atlantic bluefin tuna – but a quite different fate had been set for you and your kind even then.

Your metallic blue back contrasts sharply with your silvery abdomen. Muscular you are and nimble; with powerful, short strokes of the tailfin you can reach almost 70 km/h over short distances.

As a large predator you are high up the food chain, flexible enough to adapt to the changing food supply offered by the oceans. If you need to you will dive as deep as a thousand metres in search of prey. Your favourite meals, however, are herring, mackerel and sardines. With their high fat content they provide the energy you need to remain in constant motion – and stopping would be the death of you since only through movement does sufficient oxygen enter your body through your gills. You can cope with conditions ranging between 3 and 30 degrees Celsius. Like us humans, you can keep your body temperature almost even; your circulatory system is extraordinary for a fish. But the same marvel that makes this possible, your network of blood vessels, also presents great challenges for the industry that has helped make you famous. '

Off the coast of Tarifa, at the southernmost tip of Spain, a good fifty fishermen are preparing for the big kill. It is mid-May. Schools of tuna are passing by the Strait of Gibraltar, and a few of the fish have become entangled in the intricately designed underwater labyrinth of gillnets anchored to the sea floor. With their boats the fishermen form a circle, while divers underwater separate out the creatures to be slaughtered today, the rest to remain in the nets until it is their turn. A light breeze from the west spreads the mild rays of the sun over the water as a signal comes from below. The divers have chosen the catch. They drive the fish towards the *copo*, a sturdy net from which there is no escape. Back on the surface the boats now move closer and closer together until they are side by side. The trap is closed and well filled.

The next signal from the divers changes the atmosphere instantly – especially on the ship from which the *patrón*, who is in charge here, roars his orders. '*Arria, arria, vira, vira, iza, iza,*' the fishermen shout urgently in their

ROCÍO PUNTAS BERNET is a Spanish journalist who grew up in Tarifa, where her love of the sea was born. She is co-founder of the Swiss bi-monthly investigative magazine *Reportagen*, and her articles have been published in the Spanish daily *ABC* as well as the Swiss weekly *NZZ am Sonntag*. Since 2019 she has directed the programme of the True Story Festival in Bern, an event, organised by *Reportagen*, dedicated to international journalism.

LAURA LEÓN GÓMEZ is a multi-award-winning Spanish photographer and video-maker. Her work has focused primarily on Europe, Africa and Asia for publications such as *The New York Times*, *El País Semanal*, *M: Le Magazine du Monde*, *Vanity Fair*, *Der Spiegel* and *Time* as well as for the Warner TV and Discovery Channel television networks. Her photographs have been reproduced in numerous books and some are held in private collections and by national foundations.

almadraba slang, calling for the nets to be released and hauled in. The men in their bright-orange waterproofs seem to be everywhere at once, their movements nimble and precise. The net is drawn ever tighter, and the water, up to now calm, suddenly bursts into life. It churns and bubbles, while beneath the surface dark shadows dart back and forth between the boats. The bluefin tuna are in turmoil and do not understand where this powerful net is taking them as it is pulled higher and higher, leaving them with less and less water.

Until just a few years ago the *levantá*, the raising of the net, was a far bloodier affair. 'It was like being on drugs; you felt an incredible adrenaline rush,' recalls Juan Carlos Aranda. 'Afterwards every muscle would hurt. But at the time you didn't feel anything – not how cold the water was nor the pain when you caught a blow. When we were in the water we were oblivious to everything else.' Juan Carlos used to be a *copejador*, one of the men who would throw themselves into the water to kill the tuna. As soon as the fish had appeared on the surface, the *copejadores*, would leap into the nets. The goal was to ram the hook into the tuna's eye as quickly as possible. The water level in the net would rise and fall the whole time, and the fish with it, so the *copejadores* would have to get their timing exactly right to catch them. 'If you got one, you would have to heave it on to the boat somehow,' Juan

Carlos remembers. 'There were fish that weighed half a tonne and were up to three metres long.' The whole process was far quicker back then than it is today. Nevertheless, it was, of course, still stressful for the fish. In the boat they would lash out with their tail fins until they were dead. Juan Carlos imitates the movement of a fish thrashing itself, making a sound like the 'clap, clap, clap' of loud applause – but this applause damages the fish's valuable flesh in a way that goes beyond any surface wound. Long periods of stress cause lactic acid to be produced in the muscles. This imparts to the meat an unpleasant metallic taste – a phenomenon known in Japanese as *yake*, burned-meat syndrome – and makes it unsuitable for consumption raw.

As soon as the net is raised it is time for the divers to go back in. Three remain on the surface of the water with a short-barrelled underwater gun at the ready. The cartridges are fired only on contact to avoid the risk of missing. The divers drift face down in the sea like corpses. Patiently they wait until they have their victim before them at the optimal angle. The shot between the eyes must be perfectly aimed to avoid any chance of missing, which would cause the fish to try to escape or wound it in a way that would mean wasting some of the precious meat. The two other divers set about heaving the fish out of the net, and Juan Carlos, who today operates the

Annual catch by country, average 2018–20

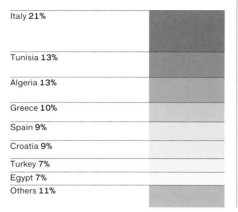

Italy **21%**

Tunisia **13%**

Algeria **13%**

Greece **10%**

Spain **9%**

Croatia **9%**

Turkey **7%**

Egypt **7%**

Others **11%**

Annual catch by species, average 2018–20

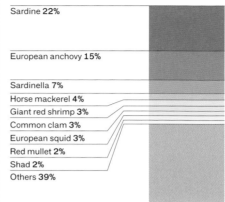

Sardine **22%**

European anchovy **15%**

Sardinella **7%**

Horse mackerel **4%**

Giant red shrimp **3%**

Common clam **3%**

European squid **3%**

Red mullet **2%**

Shad **2%**

Others **39%**

Annual turnover for the first sale of fishery products in the top seven Mediterranean and Black Sea producing countries, by type of fisheries, 2020, millions of dollars

Small-scale fishing Industrial fishing

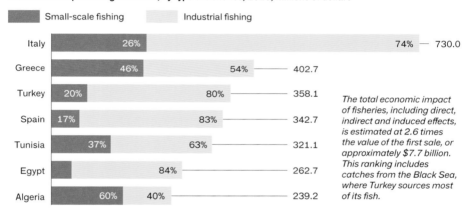

Italy	26%	74% — 730.0
Greece	46%	54% — 402.7
Turkey	20%	80% — 358.1
Spain	17%	83% — 342.7
Tunisia	37%	63% — 321.1
Egypt		84% — 262.7
Algeria	60%	40% — 239.2

The total economic impact of fisheries, including direct, indirect and induced effects, is estimated at 2.6 times the value of the first sale, or approximately $7.7 billion. This ranking includes catches from the Black Sea, where Turkey sources most of its fish.

Major fishing ports in the Mediterranean, 2021 (2020 data for Tunisia and 2018 for Egypt), thousands of tonnes per annum

16.6 Izbat Al Burj (Egypt)

16.4 Chebba (Tunisia)

14.5 Téboulba (Tunisia)

13.7 Port Said (Egypt)

11.4 Ghazaouet (Algeria)

10.6 Burullus (Egypt)

10.3 Kélibia (Tunisia)

8.9 Sfax (Tunisia)

8.7 Chioggia (Italy)

8.3 Zarzis (Algeria)

73%

of commercial fish stocks in the Mediterranean and Black Sea are exploited above sustainability levels, but pressure on stocks decreased by 21% from 2013 to 2022 (and by 10% from 2020 to 2022).

SOURCE: FAO

crane, hoists them on deck where the *coup de grâce* will be administered using the *ikejime* method. After the brain is spiked a thin wire is inserted, which penetrates the spinal column and immediately cuts off all neural activity. In this way *yake* is avoided and the quality of the meat remains uncompromised. A further incision is made below the dorsal fin to drain the warm blood.

With fish hanging motionless beside him, Juan Carlos, a man of forty-eight, looks tiny. He pauses for a moment, humble before the giant creatures, and then they are taken off to an ice-filled hold. Just a few moments later the Japanese representative, who was standing alongside the *patrón* during the lifting of the nets watching the spectacle with a serious expression, gives the order to load the first batch of tuna on to the Japanese refrigerated freighter, anchored not far from the *almadraba*, for storage at minus 70 degrees Celsius until their arrival in Japan.

In the 1980s the Japanese freighter would still call at the port of Tarifa, and the whole village used to await the huge vessel's arrival. The ships at that time would arrive in spring, a few days before the schools of wild bluefin tuna, which, following their instincts, would make their way from the North Atlantic to spawn in the warmer waters of the Mediterranean where they had first come into the world. The Japanese were not the first to think of catching tuna on their way through the Strait of Gibraltar. Neolithic people had done the same thing more than five thousand years before, as evidenced by paintings in the Cueva de las Orcas, the cave named after the killer whales that are the tuna's only natural enemy.

The Phoenicians, too, who settled the

THE UNITED NATIONS OF CRIME

Marbella, at the heart of the Costa del Sol, is home to almost 150,000 people and a property market more inflated than that of Madrid. This came about because in the 1960s, under Franco, it became a tourist destination for a very select clientele, high-ranking criminals, on the proviso that they brought their money with them but left the violence at home. And so it was for many years. Marbella enjoys a strategic location for drug trafficking: a narrow tongue of the Mediterranean separates it from Ceuta and Melilla, sources of Moroccan hashish; it is only a few kilometres from the tax haven of Gibraltar; and the mountains of Andalusia are the principal base for marijuana cultivation in Europe. Then on its doorstep you have the Atlantic, with its cargoes of South American cocaine, so over the years organised-crime groups from all over the world have found it to be a vital hub for trafficking as well a place to cohabit peacefully with international 'colleagues', a sort of free market (which even attracts seasonal workers) for services associated with the drugs trade, from transport to money laundering, with no cartels or territorial boundaries. Recently, however, minor and middle-ranking criminals have started to arrive and frequently resort to violence without feeling the need to hide from an under-resourced local police force. And so the situation has changed, and shootings and score-settling are frequent occurrences, to the extent that even the bosses no longer feel safe: 'There's no code any more, no respect any more,' one of them complained in an interview.

eastern Mediterranean coast in modern-day Syria, Lebanon and Israel in the first millennium BCE, would wait for tuna in the Strait of Gibraltar; the art of *almadraba* goes back to them – an art that the Romans perfected and that the Arabs also practised. However, the red-meat boom did not come until the 20th century, when Japanese immigrants brought their favourite fish dishes with them to their new homes in the West, especially the USA. Sushi in particular has grown in popularity since the 1990s; it had an easy time winning over consumers who were not only open to anything new, unfamiliar and exotic but also increasingly interested in eating healthily. Fish used for the raw delicacy have to meet stringent requirements – and the bluefin tuna is unequalled in the

extent to which it possesses the qualities sought. The trend for imported foods led to a surge in demand for red tuna; the consequences were soon felt.

By 2007 Atlantic bluefin tuna had declined dramatically from peak stocks to 28 per cent on the Atlantic east coast and to 18 per cent on the west coast. ICCAT, the International Commission for the Conservation of Atlantic Tunas, was compelled to intervene and impose a tough plan for population recovery. In its first few years fishing quotas were reduced to such an extent that the entire industry groaned under the harsh cuts. The past three years have seen a relaxation, and quotas have been raised from 20,000 to 36,000 tonnes. While bluefin tuna is still on the verge of extinction in the Pacific, it is believed that at least the

Opposite: Fishermen raise their nets in Zahara de los Atunes, Cadiz.
Above: The tuna are surrounded by nets and boats as the hunt reaches its climax.

Atlantic east coast now has a healthy and stable population. The big unknown factor, and the one that could tip the scales, is illegal fishing, which could quickly upset the delicate balance once more.

' I'm standing beside you, just a few metres away, and I'd love to touch you, your smooth, clean skin. It is not actually cold, but when the master cutter known as "the snorer" enters the room with something completely different in mind the air freezes. He holds a knife in his right hand and a hook in his left with which he will bring all two hundred kilograms of you into position as required. When the knife hits your spine, you make this very special sound that gives the art of tuna cutting and filleting its name in Spanish, *el ronqueo*, a kind of snoring or hoarse roaring. The snorer first removes your caudal fin, then your head. Then he takes away the soft roe – you can see what a powerful little man you were. From the stomach the white fillets are cut away and the dark ones from the back. After that the *ventresca*, your most precious meat, is removed, its fat content of 10 per cent considered optimal for the Japanese consumer, followed by the dark upper parts, the *descargamentos*, and the lean belly meat, the *tarantelo*.

'No one cares where you've come from. As quickly as possible you will be flown to the world's most demanding markets or shipped across the world's oceans at minus 70 degrees.'

Every little piece of you is picked off. Even the jelly of your eyes ends up in a cocktail. Not for nothing are you called the "pig of the seas".

Although you have just one "high season", when schools of you pass by here off the coast of southern Spain, high demand means that you are not allowed a break at any other time of year but instead are caught, locked up and fattened, just as pigs or geese are on the land. If there is a *before-and-after-Covid-19* for us humans, then there is a *before-and-after-the-sushi-hype* for you.

Yes, I know – even green asparagus has it better than you. Asparagus, at least, comes with a label of origin to draw attention to the long transport routes and thus the climate-change implications of importing it to Europe out of season from Mexico or Peru. But you? No one cares where you've come from. As quickly as possible you will be flown to the world's most demanding markets or shipped across the world's oceans at minus 70 degrees. **❯**

Today not all the tuna caught at the *almadraba* goes to Japan. Gadira, the company that markets the fish caught at three of the four *almadrabas* off the coast of Spain's Cádiz region, keeps half of the catch for itself. After years of doing business with Japan, the company has learned a good deal from the Japanese way of doing things. Processes have been optimised; methods have been adopted. Butchering the tuna, for example, is far more productive if done the Japanese way.

Gadira's methods have enabled the company to free itself from the restrictions of the tuna-spawning cycle and meet high year-round demand, while also regulating the market price by not having to put all its stock on to the market at the same time. The company went into 2020 expecting a strong year. With ICCAT having granted it a higher fishing quota of 1,100 tonnes of bluefin tuna, things were looking good. Until March. Until the virus came along. The strict lockdown unleashed a chain of fears. Would they be allowed to fish at all? Would the Japanese come to Spain when borders were closed? And even if they were able to fish, how would they sell their catch when the entire hotel-and-catering sector was paralysed?

The tuna-fishing villages normally hold *rutas del atún* (tuna routes) festivals, important marketing events at bars and restaurants in which the growing popularity of different forms of sushi has made it increasingly difficult to make an impression with traditional local recipes. These had to be cancelled. However, something unexpected happened: customers, determined to get their tuna, far from surrendering to the uncertainty, went straight to their smartphones and used them to order the coveted red meat. Gadira reacted swiftly, and an online shop was quickly set up. The promise: to deliver to any location on the Iberian Peninsula within forty-eight hours. The pandemic opened up completely new ways of selling to a market that was already unstoppable.

In the Mediterranean region alone tuna fishing generates more than €1 billion annually. Such a lucrative resource inevitably triggers conflicts of interest between the nations among which the fishing quotas are divided. Norway and Denmark, for example, are calling for an increased catch quota in view of a recovery of the bluefin tuna populations in their waters. In addition, there are countries, such as Mauritania or Namibia, where tuna are now being sighted for the first time or the first time in a long time, and they, too, want to be allowed to catch the fish, which do, after all, feed in their waters. Others, such as Japan, on the other hand, insist on their historical rights. And then there is the United Nations agreement obliging industrialised nations – including the EU member states, the USA and Canada – to cede part of their quotas to emerging nations such as Morocco.

For bluefin tuna Spain has the highest fishing quota of any nation. In 2020 this amounted to almost six thousand tonnes, one sixth of the globally permitted total. The bulk is caught by fleets that fish using purse seines – deep encircling nets used to surround a school of fish. The Spanish fleets are mainly in the hands of two families, the Fuentes in Murcia and the Balfegó in Tarragona. Only after the next largest share has gone to the *almadrabas* do the more than one thousand small-scale fishing vessels get a look-in. Ordinary fishermen are left with a miserable quota with which they barely manage to make ends meet – either that or they just give up.

At the port of Tarifa, Manuel Suárez prepares for the next trip out. The thirty-four-year-old originally studied sports, not wanting to have anything to do with fishing, but in the end became a fisherman like his uncle and grandfather – and was even elected chairman of the fishermen's guild. Standing up for colleagues' rights is no simple task, and nor is tackling the problems of the industry, of which there are many. 'Obtaining higher fishing quotas is anything but easy. After all, not everyone is allowed to fish what and where they want,' he says. The quota calculations are based on the number of catches made to date and the size of the vessels as well as how long a fisherman has been engaged in tuna fishing. 'Suppose the son of a fisherman also wants to get into the business but doesn't yet have any catches of his own, then he doesn't stand a chance, and yet so much is at stake for him,' says Manuel, and the very elderly sailor next to him, his skin more wrinkled than a dried fig, nods in agreement as he winds up his fishing lines.

Manuel complains that the Spanish authorities have completely written the agricultural and fisheries sectors off and only local government still supports them. Meanwhile, he adds, significantly more young people are interested in fishing today than a few years ago, even though fish stocks have declined. Off Tarifa it was mainly red bream that used to be caught, but these are no longer to be found, partly because they have been overfished and partly because the few that do remain form a much-favoured part of the tuna's diet.

The social impact on young people is quite severe, says Manuel. As a rule, young fishermen do not have the means to buy another fisherman's quota. To make matters worse, they see tuna

Rafael Márquez, captain of
a fishing boat, poses in the
fishery company's warehouse
in Barbate, Cadiz.

but are not allowed to touch them –
even though the tuna cause huge problems for them by eating all the other
fish that are left. It doesn't help that
the young Spaniards know that Moroccan fishermen off the coast opposite are
making catch after catch. 'And as if that
weren't enough, we're also struggling
with a plague of Asian algae,' complains
Manuel. The mood is low, and the young
fishermen are constantly in dispute with
one another.

Some secretly switch to illegal paths
instead. If you're looking for tuna in
Tarifa you don't have to look that hard –
it almost literally swims into your house.
'Of course, one of my son's friends has
one right now. My husband's uncle
knows someone who ... for three or four
or six euros a kilo. Is it fresh, you ask? Of
course. It comes straight from the sea.'
The only problem is that nobody knows
how long the fish has been dead in the
water or dragged along by a boat. Raúl
García, fisheries specialist at the World
Wide Fund for Nature (WWF), confirms
that the situation in Tarifa is fraught
with conflict and that the industry is
running on empty. 'Some people barely
get by with the legal quotas they bring in
during the day, and then at night they go
out again and continue fishing illegally.'

Illegally caught tuna causes numerous problems for the market. For

THE GREAT REPLACEMENT

The legendarily intense Mediterranean blue is not just an emotional impression or an Instagram filter, it is the visual effect of the sea's oligotrophic state, in other words the lack of dissolved nutrients that would 'spoil' its colour. Apart from the mouths of the big rivers, with their vibrant ecosystems and large numbers of endemic species that make them biodiversity hotspots, the Mediterranean tends to be relatively lacking in life, particularly in its eastern quadrant. But it is also a sea undergoing a transformation, partly because it is heating up faster than other parts of the globe, leading to a phenomenon of tropicalisation, the process whereby tropical species (plants and animals) establish themselves after entering via the Strait of Gibraltar or the Suez Canal. In the latter case they are known as 'Lessepsian species', after the French diplomat Ferdinand de Lesseps who was behind the construction of the canal, and they account for the majority of the thousand or so invasive species. Intermingling is not bad in itself, but the behaviours of certain Lessepsian species, such as the silver-cheeked toadfish (which grazes on the *Posidonia* on the seabed) or the scorpion fish (which feeds on the larvae of other species), are harmful to the host ecosystem. Other invasive species, however, such as the blue crab (which actually comes from the Atlantic) have become new resources for fishermen. And then there are those, such as the stone bass, that, perhaps fed up with the new arrivals, have made the journey in the opposite direction, taking the much less popular anti-Lessepsian route from the Mediterranean to the Red Sea.

example, a high-quality piece of legally caught tuna, at €80 a kilo, cannot compete with the significantly lower prices charged for illegal catches. The lower prices become possible only if regulations are not adhered to and the associated costs are thus avoided. The cold chain, for example, can be dispensed with. After all, without hygiene controls, the fish does not have to be kept quite as fresh. The meat may lose some of its deep-red colour, but beetroot juice can make it attractive to a buyer again in no time. (The same trick is also used to turn other tuna species into bluefin and then sell them at a suitably high price.) Anyone who consumes unhygienically stored fish risks ending up in hospital with severe food poisoning. If this happens the rest of the degraded fish is immediately withdrawn from the market. Those who fish illegally tend not to make a point of using QR codes to ensure the tuna's traceability from catch to consumer. If traceability guidelines were rigorously followed by all parties involved there would be very few opportunities for illegal fishing, and the black market in tuna would be history.

With the legal fishing of bluefin tuna, according to WWF's Raúl García, the biggest problem is the fattening farms and the cages in which the fish are dragged along to them. The animals are caught with huge purse seines and diverted into floating cages, which are then dragged to the fattening facilities by tugboats at a minimum speed of just one knot. The fish can thus swim along without either crushing one another or being pressed against the net by its forward motion. Although the process is closely monitored with the aid of underwater cameras – and in particularly suspect cases

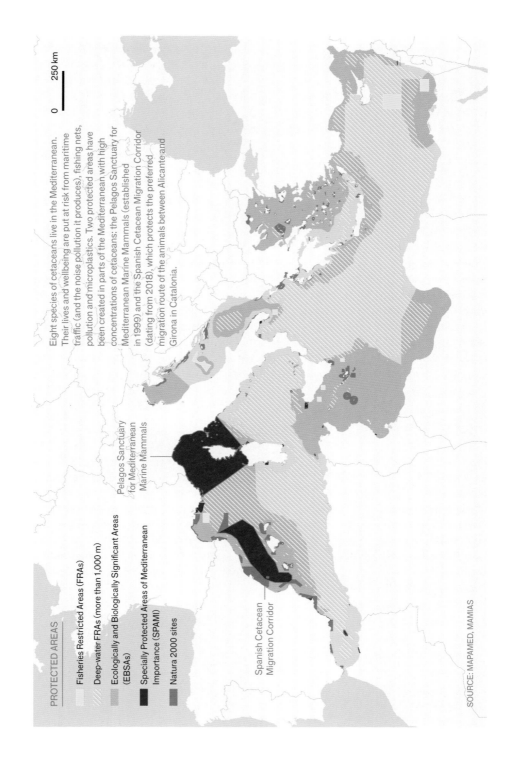

PROTECTED AREAS

Fisheries Restricted Areas (FRAs)

Deep-water FRAs (more than 1,000 m)

Ecologically and Biologically Significant Areas (EBSAs)

Specially Protected Areas of Mediterranean Importance (SPAMI)

Natura 2000 sites

Pelagos Sanctuary for Mediterranean Marine Mammals

Spanish Cetacean Migration Corridor

Eight species of cetaceans live in the Mediterranean. Their lives and wellbeing are put at risk from maritime traffic (and the noise pollution it produces), fishing nets, pollution and microplastics. Two protected areas have been created in parts of the Mediterranean with high concentrations of cetaceans: the Pelagos Sanctuary for Mediterranean Marine Mammals (established in 1999) and the Spanish Cetacean Migration Corridor (dating from 2018), which protects the preferred migration route of the animals between Alicante and Girona in Catalonia.

0   250 km

SOURCE: MAPAMED, MAMIAS

'Without hygiene controls, the fish does not have to be kept quite as fresh. The meat may lose some of its deep-red colour, but beetroot juice can make it attractive to a buyer again in no time.'

even accompanied by television cameras – it is extremely difficult, with the fish in constant motion, for the inspector on board the ship to estimate their number or individual weights.

In addition, one can never be sure that another, illegal catch will not be later added to the legal, supervised one. This is relatively easy to do, especially in countries such as Malta, Tunisia or Morocco, where controls are generally less stringent. When the catch is sold the farmers can explain how heavy it is by claiming that the fish have gained significantly more weight than expected at the fattening stage. Operation Tarantelo, which was coordinated by Europol in 2018, discovered farmers who claimed that their tuna had increased in weight by 60 per cent in just three months – which is a physical impossibility.

'I've seen you frolicking in the sea. I've seen you chopped into bite-sized pieces. And now I'm going to swim with you. The Tuna Tour involves a catamaran excursion, including a forty-five-minute swim with you, followed by a tasting of your exquisite meat. However, this is no tourist attraction, according to Joan from the marketing department. Rather, the Tuna Tour is intended to show how you live, how you eat; it is intended to bring us humans closer to your way of life and is thus to be regarded less as an excursion and more of a "point of communication". Just like the Barcelona restaurant of the Balfegó tuna brand, the Tunateca, with fish scale decorations and chairs as red as your meat.

It's 10 o'clock in the morning, and the August sun is burning down mercilessly. Families with young children, who don't look too enthusiastic, board the catamaran. After twenty minutes' sailing the catamaran stops next to one of the cages – or "tanks", as the Tuna Tour calls them – in which you and the other tuna are forced to swim. There are fifteen thousand fish here in twenty-one tanks, says Joan. The wind stirs the sea; the water is not particularly clear. First a diver descends into the pool; she must check if everything is in order. Visitors to the "point of communication" queue before the narrow ladder that leads down into the pool. With diving goggles and snorkels, they now descend one at a time.

Not one of you has yet shown up to greet the visitors, and no wonder. I, too, would not voluntarily welcome my executioner. Now the crew of the catamaran start to pour sardinellas – a type of sardine that is inedible to humans but an irresistible treat for you because of its high fat content – into the water. Like rockets launched from the bottom of the sea, you emerge at the water's surface. We are assured that you will avoid any touch because we frighten you and because the contact would hurt your delicate skin, but I still think it best to keep away from the points at which the feed hits the water.

The next time I submerge my head I see one of you right below me. So close, so big. Because I don't have a snorkel I come up for air. When I look down again you've gone. 🟊

A thousand kilometres from Tarifa, halfway between Valencia and Barcelona, is the fishing village of L'Ametlla de Mar, where the Balfegó family runs its business. Like many other families in Spain, the Balfegós were traditional fishermen for many generations, but today they dedicate themselves to industrial fishing. This year their purse seine fleet managed to catch their full year's allocation of 2,240 tonnes within seventy-two hours. Each fish brought in by their nets weighs on average 150 kilograms. In the cages of their farm, where they are then fattened for months, the 2,240 tonnes will have increased considerably by the time the fat content has reached the levels demanded by the thirty-two countries to which Balfegó exports its fish. And Balfegó continues to grow, its turnover exceeding €50 million in 2018.

Listening to Joan Grau, the twenty-eight-year-old head of marketing and communications at the company, you could mistake him for a born politician. Eloquent and smooth when discussing the company's successes, reserved when it comes to the less pleasant questions. Joan speaks of the company as 'we' and takes issue with the vocabulary used for tuna-related matters – 'We'd rather speak of feeding than fattening.' By keeping the fish in tanks Balfegó is able to deliver fresh produce 365 days a year, with divers ready to go in and bring out fish to order. Joan insists that they do not run a fattening farm but keep wild tuna, 'because we fish them off the Balearic Islands and we feed them from June, when they are caught, until at least September. What they eat during this time makes up for the 30 per cent of fat they lost on their way from the North Atlantic to the Mediterranean. We give them herring and mackerel – exactly what they would eat in the wild.'

However, it's not just tuna who eat these; the entire marine ecosystem depends on these supplies of fish. In Raúl García's eyes enormous resources are being squandered here, with fish that have traditionally been part of a human diet thrown into insatiable giant mouths just to maintain a luxury market. 'Ten-to-twelve kilos of fish are needed for a tuna to gain just one kilo – that's madness,' says the WWF environmentalist. 'Europe imports masses of fish from Africa – high-quality, expensive fish. Conversely, we export one-to-two million tonnes of mackerel – a fish that is less expensive and thus affordable for African markets, but nevertheless highly nutritious. And now the tuna companies are coming along and joining the scramble for mackerel, in competition with countries like Nigeria and Ghana.'

The events of January 2020 revealed a further, previously unknown, dark side to the fattening farms. When Storm Gloria battered the Tarragona region on Spain's east coast, the strong swell caused the Balfegó cages to spill, and about twelve thousand tuna escaped from the facilities. Along the entire coast, hundreds of tonnes of rotten fish were washed up on the shores, having been injured and killed during the storm. Worse still, some fish became caught in the nets, spoiling the entire catch. Balfegó offered to compensate the affected fishermen and now claim they have done everything possible to resolve the issue. The fishermen, however, have yet to receive any compensation.

Balfegó's image is dependent on the

'Some restaurateurs proudly say that their tuna comes from Balfegó, of course; others admit in a hushed voice that they would only buy from Balfegó if they could not get anything else, and that they would rather support traditional fishermen.'

outcome of the compensation payments and whether the company takes measures to prevent a repeat of the mass loss of tuna. A drop in prestige would be a bitter pill for Balfegó, and so concerned is the company to preserve its reputation that it barely gave Operation Tarantelo time to get under way before making clear that it had nothing to do with the whole affair – and even acted alongside Greenpeace in taking out a private prosecution against a direct competitor and dozens of others within the industry. It is not surprising then that a range of opinions about Balfegó are to be found in L'Ametlla de Mar. The man from the tourist information office, for example, enthuses about the Tuna Tour, as do Balfegó's employees and their families. Some restaurateurs proudly say that their tuna comes from Balfegó, of course; others admit in a hushed voice that they would only buy from Balfegó if they could not get anything else, and that they would rather support traditional fishermen. There are reports that trucks full of frozen squid, said to serve as food for the tuna in the fattening facilities, give off such a stench as they pass by that several restaurants have complained and made sure that the trucks now take a different route. Then again, to return to the Tuna Tour, tourists are enraptured by the unique experience of swimming with the fish.

Then there are those who see the cages posing a whole range of other problems. Joan Argento, forty-three, looks more like a tourist than an experienced fisherman, with his bright eyes, shorts, T-shirt, sandals and baseball cap featuring the flag of his wife's home country, Bulgaria. With a cigarillo in his mouth, busy unloading boxes of fresh fish, he says he simply can't understand why no one is willing to open their eyes. 'All you need to do is follow the trail of the birds, and you'll see the tuna jumping. I've been here for a good twenty years now, but I've never seen anything like it. The tuna are attracted by the captive tuna and the food that spills out of the cages. And then they just stay and grab what few fish we have left.' As predators, tuna have also scared away other fish.

If it were up to Joan Argento the NGOs would have to look into the matter. 'If this were widely known then they would certainly increase the quota for us individual fishermen.' Not even fifty tonnes has been allocated to the entire coast of Tarragona, Argento complains. The competitive situation that this creates among fishermen is unnatural: first come, first served. What also worries him is the waste from the cages. 'Hundreds of fish that eat and excrete vast amounts – where will that lead? I'm a longline fisher, and these days, when I haul in the line, there's always some kind of mush caught on it. That didn't happen before the cages.'

This operation, a joint effort between the Spanish Guardia Civil and Europol, was named after one of the most highly prized parts of the tuna, taken from the upper part of the fish's belly. The investigations, which also involved Portugal, France, Malta and Italy, began in 2017, when it was discovered that a cargo of contraband tuna was the cause of a series of food-poisoning outbreaks. A year later they were able to arrest seventy-nine people and confiscate eighty tonnes of illegal fish from Italy and Malta that was heading for the Spanish market. According to the Spanish authorities the traffic was managed by a criminal organisation well versed in muddying the waters and operating between legality and illegality. Pulling the strings was, allegedly, the Cartagena-based firm Ricardo Fuentes e Hijos, the world's largest tuna trader no less and also the owner of the Mare Blu fish farm in Malta, another operation involved in the investigations. Research by the website *El Confidencial* revealed that the then director of Malta's department of fisheries, Andreina Fenech Farrugia, who was later removed from office, was in the pocket of the tuna racketeers. The island nation has been reprimanded several times by the European Commission for negligence in monitoring the sector. With a capacity of twelve thousand tonnes, Malta is the leader in the tuna-fattening industry, which is also one of the country's main sources of foreign revenue. The five floating cage farms a few kilometres off the coast are stocked with fish caught mainly by Italian and French fishermen that are then relocated to Malta.

It is not only what the tuna excrete that ends up at the bottom of the sea but also the indigestible parts of the fish they consume – bones, for example. For Fernando de la Gándara, director of the Institute of Oceanography (IEO) in Mazarrón in the province of Murcia, southwest of Valencia, the solution clearly lies in replacing fresh fish with cattle feed, which would result in significantly less waste. Fernando has been trying to domesticate tuna for years; he knows the fish inside out, and he knows why they are so downright cautious. Although they have muscles like bulls, their skeleton is no more resistant than that of a sardine, which means they don't resist when they realise that they are trapped in a net. A sign of fear? Or intelligence?

Tuna have been found to have a memory and to get angry at sounds they don't like, and when they are angry they stop eating. In their behaviour, Fernando says, tuna in captivity hardly differ from their wild counterparts. The only thing they lose is the instinct to travel. Their instincts also tell them to flee when they are nervous, which is also one of the great problems of captivity – preventing the animals from crashing against the cage bars and killing themselves.

In 2016, when full-cycle tuna farming was achieved for the first time, EU support had already been secured for another, even more ambitious project: the controlled breeding of bluefin tuna in artificial conditions. A ship specially designed for the project stands in the immediate vicinity of the beach of Mazarrón and houses four tanks with a water capacity of seven million litres and shiny walls that increase their visibility to the fish and make it less likely

Quartering, one of the many bloody stages in the process of tuna butchery.

that they will crash into them and be killed.

Since they always have food to eat and do not have to look for it, farmed tuna grow faster than in the wild. Although all fish are from the same year, you can recognise by their size the individuals that prevail in the fight for food. When it gets colder towards winter, the water is heated to prevent unnecessary energy consumption by the tuna. To manipulate the reproductive cycle, interference with light conditions and water temperature tricks the fish into thinking it is summer in the middle of December. The stress that the tuna seem to suffer when they reproduce in captivity is neutralised by injecting a hormone.

Economically, the breeding of bluefin tuna is not profitable, Fernando admits; however, he expects it to provide valuable knowledge about the species that will help optimise its capture and keep. The knowledge gained can then be passed on to commercial enterprises. He also believes that a controllable reproductive cycle would bring a significant recovery to fishing grounds, thus securing stocks for future generations.

This is also what JC Mackintosh is striving for. The company is expanding with a completely new technique for fishing tuna that has astonished the entire fishing guild along the strait. In

A selection of raw-tuna dishes
at a restaurant in Barbate.

2015 Juan Carlos Mackintosh, a native
of Malaga, travelled to Japan to learn
how to catch, slaughter and handle tuna
without losing quality between catch
and sale. Back in Spain he rounded up a
small team and got into the tuna business. Juan Carlos had an ace up his
sleeve when he returned: the green-stick
technique, a Japanese fishing method
that is considered sustainable even by
NGOs. The method involves a ship with
a twelve-metre mast, and the tuna are
lured with fish bait or silicone squid left
floating on the surface of the water. 'In
the beginning the other fishermen made
fun of us,' recalls elder son Daniel. 'They
didn't believe that it would work, that
the tuna would really snap at the colourful squid. If the quotas were higher, we
could fish here all year round,' he adds.
In the meantime, the next innovation is
already on the horizon: JC Mackintosh is
banking on smoked bluefin tuna to take
off in the future – a culinary novelty not
even the Japanese had thought of.

❛ The starting signal for the 2019
bluefin *ruta* in Tarifa was given in
the medieval chapel of the Castillo
de Guzmán el Bueno – which brings me
a little closer to you, because this is
where I got married. It's the beginning
of a ten-day festival with fifty-two completely different, multi-faceted tapas

The growing global demand for animal proteins is one of the great challenges of the 21st century. While some see vegetarianism or insects as the answer, the UN Food and Agriculture Organization – perhaps more realistically, and in spite of all the environmental and dietary problems that it generates – believes that aquaculture is one solution. The Mediterranean, where extensive farms in lagoons and intensive farms in cages coexist, is playing its part; while fishing is down dramatically since its peak in the 1990s, aquaculture has quadrupled since then, and in 2020 it accounted for more than 40 per cent of fish production. The two biggest fish-farming countries in the Mediterranean are Egypt and Turkey, which together account for around half the market by value, followed at some distance by Greece, Italy and Spain. Italy specialises in mussels, raising around two-thirds of the Mediterranean's total production, but the species that dominate Mediterranean fish farming are the sea bass and sea bream. More than 95 per cent of global production of these two fish comes from aquaculture, of which 97 per cent comes from the Mediterranean, mainly Turkey and Greece, with the biggest consumers being Spain, France, Italy, Greece and Turkey. Egypt is a separate discussion. It pretty much has a monopoly on mullet, but, above all, it raises Nile tilapia for the internal market and for export to Asian markets, an activity that, to judge from a bas-relief in an Egyptian tomb dating from 2500 BCE, was practised in the region long before it was encouraged by the FAO.

designed to bring guests closer to all the splendour of your meat. You are the king in this competition and at the same time the only participant who has nothing to gain. In front of the church the happy invitees and the expectant journalists mingle with their notepads, microphones and cameras.

The tapas on display are so spectacular, colourful and elegant that even you would be surprised. In some bars attempts are made to blend traditional local recipes with Japanese cuisine: *ensalada rusa* with tuna tartare, tuna and foie gras, braised tuna tartare, tuna with beef from the typical red cows of Cádiz. Others opt for more exotic tapas and ingredients such as sesame, ginger, wasabi, soya sauce, seaweed, red fruits, mango or avocado.

One by one the chefs now present their plates, some in the charming dialect of Tarifa, others with Italian or French or English accents. The members of the jury stand in front of the plates, programme in hand, not knowing where to start with the tasting. You make gastronomy and tourism flourish. They've always had you here, but they didn't appreciate you until recently. Today, for better or for worse, everyone knows what you are – the red gold of the Mediterranean. 〉 🖋

The Cicadas and the Breath of the World

Is there anything more Mediterranean than succumbing to a heat-induced nap on a summer's afternoon? We follow the writer Matteo Nucci on his personal exploration of idleness to discover the kernel of truth behind this stereotype.

MATTEO NUCCI
Translated by Alan Thawley
Photography by Alessia Morellini

A slide next to the sea at the
Lidi Ferraresi, Ferrara, Italy.

It happened four years ago. I could even tell you the exact day because I filmed the scene on my phone. I had walked for two hours under a white-hot sun on one of those boiling summer mornings when all you dream of is shade, rest and a refreshing dip in the sea. But it was a long way to the beach, through almost desert-like stony fields, undulating terrain crossed by goat tracks, typical Mediterranean scrubland of juniper and mastic trees, the prickly stems of thorny burnet and every so often a larger juniper that had grown into a full-sized tree like a parasol warding off the sun. And underneath these parasols I brushed aside the tiny goat droppings covering the dusty ground and sat down to catch my breath and have a little drink before carrying on to the place where, I had been told, you could get down to a sort of amphitheatre that looks out to sea, a perfect refuge that was always deserted. And so I carried on. At a certain point, after a ravine of reddish soil where I stopped to pick up stones of a colour I had never seen before, the sea came into view, the water sparkling on a dazzling pebble beach and the sound of the waves masked by the cicadas' incredible song. I had never heard anything like it. Later, when I was telling this story, one woman offered a scientific explanation, telling me that every

seventeen years the cicadas reproduce *en masse*, which results in a surge in the population of these insects that have always captured the imagination, and their song becomes overwhelming. But that kind of explanation leaves me cold. There was something miraculous about what I heard. Perhaps it was more to do with how tired I had been that morning, the sea that seemed like a reward and the absolute silence that reigned over the bay. But since that day, every time I hear cicadas singing, even only a few of them, I have the same impression. That their song is like regular breathing, rising and falling in time and appearing to echo the breaking of the waves on the shore. More than chirping, we could compare it to the lowing of cattle. Like the sound of a fantastic bull-like beast formed from the myriad cicadas in the world. It was that very morning when everything realigned, and I had a sense of finally being able to grasp the meaning of the sea beside which I was born and raised.

Of course, nothing would have been possible without a thousand previous experiences. The most important (or perhaps the most emblematic) took place on a winter's day at a Greek workshop in Piraeus. It was one of those large, dilapidated garages where all you can see at night are the grey shutters

MATTEO NUCCI is a Roman author who has studied ancient philosophy and published essays on Empedocles, Socrates and Plato, editing and translating Plato's *Symposium* for Einaudi. His first novel, *Sono comuni le cose degli amici* (Ponte alle Grazie, 2009), was shortlisted for the Strega Prize, as was *È giusto obbedire alla notte* (Ponte alle Grazie, 2017). More recent works include *Achille e Odisseo: La ferocia e l'inganno* (Einaudi, 2020), *Sono difficili le cose belle* (HarperCollins, 2022) and *Il grido di Pan* (Einaudi, 2023). His short stories have been anthologised in numerous collections, and his articles, which appear in *Il Venerdì di Repubblica* and *L'Espresso*, are available online on the cultural blog *minima&moralia*.

ALESSIA MORELLINI is an Italian freelance photographer with a passion for travel. Her early work focused on the Po Valley, but her research later took her further afield. The places she seeks out in her search for an infinite summer are those bordering the Mediterranean: the serene island beaches, the warm hues of Morocco and sunsets that touch the sea, conveying an atmosphere of peace and tranquillity that contrasts with the frenetic pace of daily life.

and crumbling walls, but in the morning they come back to life, and a whole world opens up inside. Mechanics seemingly in a universe of their own were quietly going about their business, repairing boat engines and producing highly specialised spare parts that were shipped all across the world by well-organised companies. There was a wait that day. It was unclear how long. It was not even clear who was doing what and who would take care of us. It was raining, so we decided to go and pass the time in a café. On our return things seemed to be dragging along. Then one of the mechanics, with a nonchalance that I interpreted as kindness or perhaps pity, pointed us towards a corner at the back of the garage where some old car seats had been arranged in a kind of circle. In the middle was a low table covered in cups encrusted with coffee, overflowing ashtrays and playing cards. On the floor were backgammon boards. Sitting around it were men waiting. They chatted, smoked and passed newspapers back and forth, pointing out things they had spotted. Among them was an old man who watched us for a while, then, in Greek-inflected Italian, told us not to be in a rush. *Opoios biazetai skontaftei.* Those who rush, trip over, he explained. Time, on the other hand, is important. And where better to spend it than chatting in a café? We told him that we had just been in a café around the corner, and he laughed. 'But *this* is the café. We Greeks, wherever we are, we open a café.' He settled down in his coat, then pointed to cigarettes, newspapers, biscuits, a little gas stove and *briki* for making Greek coffee, then asked us what we needed. Nothing, we replied straight away and started to chat. The old man talked about his life and asked about us, firing off questions out of the blue such as, 'Is it possible to have a happy life?' 'What is nostalgia?' 'Why do people travel?' – which is how I came to think of Socrates.

Is there a better way of using one's time than talking and asking one another the big questions? Socrates was the absolute master of this idea, and the perfect example in which the matter is specifically laid out occurs in one of Plato's dialogues entitled *Phaedrus*, which is devoted to love and the art of speaking. The setting, as always in the works of the greatest philosophical writer of all time, is fundamental. Socrates meets Phaedrus, a young man with a passion for rhetoric, as he is repeating under his breath a speech composed by Lysias, the most famous orator of his day. He wants to learn it by heart, and, because he has the written text hidden under his clothes, Socrates asks if he can listen to him reading it. Phaedrus agrees, and Socrates follows him outside the walls of Athens, doing something absolutely extraordinary because, as he immediately explains, he likes the city and is interested in people because they can talk, whereas trees

THE PASSENGER Matteo Nucci

never say anything. But nature gains the upper hand, as Phaedrus and Socrates immerse themselves in the countryside, cross the river Ilisos, find the shade of a large plane tree and sit down. It is here that Phaedrus starts reading Lysias' speech, and Socrates offers commentary, makes a speech of his own followed by another, the heat reaches its peak, the cicadas sing and time passes. More specifically, time expands and takes shape. And the shape it takes is crucial.

Generally, when we read a translation of Plato's work we come up against the word 'time'. Ancient Greek, however, has a particular term that does not simply mean 'time'. The word is *scholé* and it means 'time free from material necessities', in other words time free from what we do to support ourselves, free from work. This is the most important dimension for a human being. When time is used for work, on the other hand, the Greek language defines it in terms of the negation of *scholé*. Using the famous 'alpha privative', the vowel that negates what follows it, the Greeks refer to work as *ascholía*, in other words an 'absence of free time'. This is a fundamental concept in understanding the civilisation that originated in the Mediterranean. In the Roman world the idea was reinterpreted through the opposition between *otium* (leisure) and *negotium* (business). The Italian term *ozio* (sloth) derives from *otium*, which was increasingly reviled as equating to neglect and loss. But the positive force of the Greek

PIRAEUS SPEAKS CHINESE

The expansion of the Suez Canal in 2015 reaffirmed the Mediterranean as one of the strategic areas for maritime traffic with around two billion tonnes of cargo moved per year. Assoporti, the Italian ports association, highlights an increase in the number of Mediterranean ports that move more than a million containers a year, from twelve in 2007 to nineteen in 2017. In 2007 Gioia Tauro in southern Italy was the Mediterranean's largest port, followed by Algeciras in Spain, but that title is now held by Tangier. The sea described by Fernand Braudel and Predrag Matvejević has changed profoundly. Whereas port cities and their centres were once cultural melting pots, nowadays they are almost always detached from cities and local communities. Piraeus is an exception, having remained one of the busiest ports (the third busiest in the Mediterranean) even though it was bought in 2016 by the shipping firm Cosco, which is owned by the Chinese state. It is not the only Mediterranean port in which the Chinese have invested – they also have stakes in Valencia, Vado Ligure, Marseilles and Thessaloniki – but Piraeus is the only one to have been sold entirely to a foreign investor, and a state-owned investor at that. At least for China it seems to have generated significant profits and a dizzying increase in maritime traffic. Bearing in mind the meagre tax receipts for the Greeks, the disadvantages seem to outweigh the advantages, above all on an environmental level, even if the Chinese press does enthusiastically report about the creation of ten thousand new jobs.

> 'The extreme heat empties cities, towns and villages, turning them into metaphysical places. Anyone who really does need to go out walks along the extremely narrow margin of shade conceded by the blazing sun.'

term prevailed over its Latin equivalent, and, in fact, *scholé* is the root of a word that has subsequently appeared in every European language: school. In other words the place – whether physical or conceptual – where we spend our time not working but focusing on ourselves, on our spiritual growth, on the fundamental questions regarding the choices we have made and will make, on the path we are following. At school you grow; at work you produce.

There is no sense in which we can conceive of this dimension of freedom from material necessities in the way we have become accustomed, envisaging the passage of time as if it ran along a straight line beginning in the past, passing through the present and on into the future. We are not engaged in work for the purposes of production or looking to the future as a point of resolution and conclusion, but rather we are immersing ourselves in the present that we inhabit and our nature, as we try to understand the human race to which we belong. And, if anything, this takes place within a cycle. Free time, as defined by *scholé*, is circular.

These might seem like idle words, mere talk, and, in fact, it *is* just talk, provided we define talk, as Socrates did in *Phaedrus*, as words that are in no way vague or distant from the reality in which we live.

But we should proceed in an orderly fashion and return to Plato and his extraordinary erotic dialogue. The whole thing takes place at a time of day that will be very familiar, for its overwhelming power, to anyone who knows the Mediterranean. We are talking about those hours of a summer's day from around midday on, when the sun prevents any kind of movement. This is a part of the day that negates every law of space and time. The extreme heat empties cities, towns and villages, turning them into metaphysical places. Shutters half down, curtains closed. Anyone who really does need to go out walks along the extremely narrow margin of shade conceded by the blazing sun. This is what we call the 'motionless hour' or, better, the *controra*, the Italian term literally meaning 'counter-hour'. Because the rules of time are subverted and everything expands, it seems that nothing else can happen and no human activity has any sense any more. In fact, we really do have the sense that nature has taken over. It is no coincidence that the ancients called it 'panic hour' – and sometimes we do, too – because Pan is the god who presides over it. He is the god of all, the god of nature, the god in which man and goat combine, celebrating the instinctiveness of the human being, our predilection for coupling and reproduction, in other words celebrating the ultimate truth that we feel in our deepest recesses, that we are a part of the mortal, animal nature that populates this cosmos. With Pan we feel that we are part of an infinite cycle of births and deaths and are in touch

·

THE PASSENGER   Matteo Nucci

The Cicadas and the Breath of the World

with what was the predominant conception of time for the ancients, who absolutely did not imagine it passing in a straight line but in a circle, because they had a cyclical vision of life and believed that everything was born, grew until it reached its prime or acme (from the Greek *akmé*, meaning 'peak' or 'full bloom') and then aged and declined to the point of death, which, in turn, made space for new life.

So Pan is the god who constantly reminds us that we are not advancing *towards* progress and resolution but *through* the cosmos that we inhabit, playing our part in the cycle that is our lot and will lead on to new cycles for those who come after us. And for precisely this reason, those who continue to conceive of their lives as following a straight, productive line during the immobile hour, the counter-hour, Pan's hour, are enemies of Pan – and, let me be clear, this is a serious matter. When he sees that someone has violated the laws of nature, the goat god lets out a petrifying cry that throws people into the state of terror that takes its name from Pan himself: panic. We all know what to do when this happens: breathe, reconnect with ourselves and with the earth that supports us. But what else does all this mean if not a return to our nature and our time? The time exemplified by the Mediterranean in the radiance of summer during those hours when work is impossible.

We are now getting to the heart of an issue that is very often hurriedly dismissed, and the countries of northern Europe, the Protestant countries, are liable to condemn Mediterranean cultures precisely because of this celebration of free time. So we must be very careful. Because embracing the idea of the cycle, or circular time and the primacy of the 'scholastic', does not in any sense mean renouncing or setting aside work. If anything, it means that it is good to view work in a different spirit.

It is now time to leave the workshop in Piraeus – where, in fact, they were very hard at work, and not just because it was raining, it was winter and we were a world away from that still time of day under the influence of Pan that serves more as a paradigm. Years ago I was in southern Italy for a feature in which I was trying to describe what was left of Magna Graecia, the ancient Greek presence in Italy. I had been in Taranto, where a professor of classics had told me about what her father called 'after-lunch discussions' on the big issues, the meaning of life – in other words, everything that Plato explained in his *Phaedrus*, conversations in which you lose track of time and you embark on often surprising flights with the power to reveal obscure enigmas. I then took highway 106, heading for Crotone, once home to Pythagoras, and along the way I stopped in Cirò Marina. I wanted to see the ruins of the temple of Apollo Alaios, a few stones in the middle of a field, where Philoctetes came to enshrine his famous bow after the Trojan War. Then I headed into town to visit the museum. It was the hottest part of the day, and I had little hope of finding it open. As I suspected, it was locked up, and judging by what I could read on the weathered pieces of paper it would not reopen in the after-

'Around here, this is how we live. After lunch everyone goes to bed.' This comes from the well-known opening sequence of Lina Wertmüller's film *The Basilisks*. A voice off-camera comments on the images of a village in Basilicata where absolutely everyone, adults and children, take a nap after lunch. 'It is siesta time on a summer's day. Let's take one day at random, perhaps last year ... perhaps next year, it makes no difference.' Time is a cyclical rather than linear concept in Mediterranean civilisations. Life is a succession of cycles of sleep and wakefulness, which follows the natural cycles as far as possible – at least, until recently. Neuroscientist Matthew Walker spent a long time studying the momentous changes that occurred in Greece around the turn of the millennium, when the habit of the post-prandial nap began to wane; he found that those who gave up on siestas were 37 per cent more likely to develop cardiovascular diseases. Another study carried out by Alex Soojung-Kim Pang (2016) showed that sleeping after lunch, even for just twenty minutes, increases productivity at work. The nap has long been celebrated by famous artists and intellectuals, something that was understood by the Belgian author Georges Simenon when, in 1934, he took a long sea voyage all around the Mediterranean. Fascinated by the rituals and habits of southern Europe he wrote an account, published in *La Méditerranée en goélette* ('The Mediterranean by Schooner'), in which he describes Latin peoples as indolent and – not unreasonably – uninterested in progress.

noon. In the meantime, however, two women had stopped beside me and, perhaps struck by my disappointment, were gesturing at me to knock and ask for the attendant. I did so without much hope and more out of respect for their kindness and encouraged by their twinkling eyes. So I was surprised to see him appear straight away at the first-floor window. He was sleepy and wearing a vest, but when he understood that I was there for Apollo – the splendid head of Apollo Alaios – he got dressed and came downstairs, opened up the museum for me, turned on the lights and talked me through everything. The head was only a copy of the original, which he told me was in Reggio Calabria, but even from the reproduction you could see how perfect it was. He proudly reeled off a series of stories, beliefs and possibly invented anecdotes, and when I told him that there was no need for him to use up all his siesta time on me, he shrugged and laughed. 'We're talking,' he said, 'what

Above: The Dead Sea comes alive.
Opposite: A white shirt on a sun-lounger on the shores of the Adriatic.

of the bay. They were jumping, as goats do, probably after salt from the sea. Now Pan's here, too, I laughed, as I lay back down. The air was completely still. The amphitheatre of red earth encompassed the whole bay. The heat was intense. It felt like the summer's heat when I was a boy and there was no air conditioning, when we used to open the windows of our houses in the mornings, then they stayed closed until evening, shutters lowered, a half-light full of promises. And then, who knows why, I was reminded of Eddi.

Eddi was married to my mother's cousin Simona, on the Neapolitan side of the family. I think he was a lawyer, and he must have been a very cultured, witty man, but I don't know, as I never saw him again after he and my aunt split up. At the time I knew him I was a youngster obsessed with American Indians and pirates, and Naples was an amazing place full of mysteries. We kids were fascinated by Eddi's tales of the city. But on the day that came into my mind we weren't in Naples. We must have been in Positano, which was still a fishing village at the time, out on a Sunday get-together, perhaps in springtime, and we had to get back to Rome. The sadness was tinged with a strange euphoria, which I only experienced again as an adolescent, that ephemeral, eternal euphoria that accompanies a meal out, when everything seems possible and no one has been mean in spite of the drinking. We had gone to a trattoria

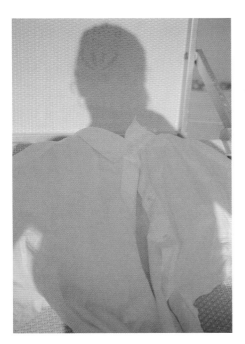

sauce, which I loved, they took us into a dark room where we had to lie down on those horrible blue folding beds, not allowed to breathe or move a muscle, we just had to sleep, and woe betide anyone who disturbed the others. For me, brimming with vitality, it was a nightmare. Itching to go out to play, run and shout, I could never get to sleep. It was genuine torture. At that point he looked at me, laughing. 'But you don't have to sleep,' he told me in that Neapolitan accent that makes everything sound simple and clear cut. 'The siesta isn't for sleeping, it's for thinking.' I looked at him. With his cigar between his teeth, his eyes shining from the wine and his black beard, he told me that he always did his thinking when he went to lie down after lunch, and I could do the same. I could think about all my pirate and Indian stories, the ones I knew, the ones I imagined, the ones I wanted to put my own twist on. I could do what I wanted in my imagination, and then, once the nap was over, I could put them into action. I really did try over the following months. My whole conception of the afternoon nap changed after I realised sleeping was not compulsory.

But back on the beach I was sleepy. The heat was too much and had exhausted me. I took out my water bottle and drank. The goats were gone. I walked over to the steep rock wall. There were small recesses in it, like little shady caves. I spread out my towel and slumped to the ground. The cicadas were singing. The sun was blazing. Their lowing was an unending cycle of breathing. Everything made sense for once. And at that point I had no more to say and no more dreams to dream. Perhaps I was succumbing to slavery; perhaps I was finally free. Whichever way, I slept. 🕊

for lunch, and everyone was in a good mood – thanks to the wine, the fish and the relaxed jokes now long-forgotten – and full of irrepressible life. My father needed to rest before getting back on the road, so I don't know where we were going, but in any case, Eddi was talking to me, laughing and making jokes, and at a certain point he passed me his cigar. 'Take it, take it,' he repeated. Everyone responded with shocked laughter, and he insisted that it was important for me to try putting the cigar in my mouth for a moment, so long as I was sure not to breathe in the smoke. It made me happy to feel so grown up. 'Now let's go and take a rest,' he said, and it seemed like the end of the world to me. I explained to him that the nap after lunch was what I hated most about school. I was doing full days at school by that time, and after the sloppy rice with tomato

An Olfactory Map

VALENTINA PIGMEI
Translated by Alan Thawley

*Truth is like the smell of the sea,
you sense it even before you see it.*
Anonymous

A study published in the journal *Frontiers in Marine Science* warns that the smell of the sea could disappear or become much less pronounced as a result of the effects of acidification. If this happens many animal species, especially molluscs, would be disorientated without the smells released by marine vegetation. I fear that the gastropods would not be alone, however; we humans would be lost, too. Smell is the sense that directs the pleasure principle, at least in my case. Without the scent of the sea I would be miserable and lost, like Dory in *Finding Nemo*.

I am hopelessly in love with the smell of the sea, with the pungent odour of its ports, where the sea breeze and brine combine with the more acrid smells of fuel, rope, the wood of the boats, fishing nets as well as with the welcoming scent of myrtle and wild oregano. But not all seas have the same smell (or colour), and those of us who have travelled by boat know, for example, that the smell changes radically near the coast. Solo sailors say that in the open water there are no smells apart from your own and that of the sea, so when you approach land you are bombarded with different aromas. Sailors also say that something changes when you enter the Mediterranean from the Atlantic, the smell of that sea is different from that of the open ocean. The Mediterranean owes its smell to substances contained in certain seaweeds (*Dictyopteris*) and marine vegetation; plants such as *Posidonia* are found nowhere else. The high level of salinity also plays its part, and the aromas of native plants – wild thyme, rosemary, myrtle, *Helichrysum*, verbena – do the rest.

THE SCENT OF THE LIGHT AND THE WIND
There is no better place to begin an olfactory journey than the long jetty in Tarifa, southern Andalusia, where the two bodies of water meet. On the one side, the blue-green Mediterranean with its low waves; on the other, the ocean with its deep, dark-blue waters and powerful smell. The contrast is marked and the scents mingle.

For family reasons I have spent a lot of time in the town of Tarifa, in the Province of Cadiz. At first I did not really understand the *gitano* charm that emerges, particularly out of season. This is borderland Spain, looking out at the Atlantic but warmed by the Mediterranean, full of contradictions like all halfway houses. Barbate, like Conil de la Frontera, Vejer de la Frontera and Jerez de la Frontera – as is easy to guess from the presence of the word 'frontier' in their names – are places that face two ways, a sort of antechamber, a transition between two possibilities: Africa and the Atlantic on the one hand and the Mediterranean on the other. The whole of the Costa de la Luz stands midway between the Mediterranean and the ocean but also between one continent and another. And, in fact, the Punta de Tarifa, as the southernmost tip of the Iberian Peninsula, is just thirteen kilometres from the African coast. This is a place where you can literally see Africa out of your window. The climate is also extreme, liminal; the wind (the Levanter) and the implacable light (from which the coast takes its name) are Mediterranean in nature but raised to the nth degree. Malù, a friend from Los Caños de Meca, was quick to warn me. What makes the

VALENTINA PIGMEI is a journalist and editorial consultant, who has worked for various Italian publishing houses. She writes about travel, books, the sea and feminism and contributes to a number of magazines, including *Vogue*, *The Vision*, *Esquire*, *Sirene*, *Cartography* and *Internazionale*. She founded the non-profit organisation La Città delle Donne (the City of Women) in Gubbio, Umbria, where she lives.

difference is the wind, she said. When the Levanter blows, and it stays for at least three or four days, life changes, women struggle with their moods and lots of people feel generally unwell. '¡Qué levantera!' the locals say on the coast. All you can do is wait for it to pass. For the portion of humanity who do not windsurf or kiteboard, the Levanter is a problem, but it is because of this wind that the mixture of scents there goes to your head. Not only do the smells of the sea and the ocean mix, the Mediterranean cuisine – the area is famous for its bluefin tuna specialities, mojama, ijada and tarantello – combines with North African spices, the smells of the fish market and the scents of Morocco along the narrow streets of white houses (see 'Red Gold' on page 141). And dominating it all is the *pinar*, the wild pine woodland that forms the vast natural park of La Breña y Marismas.

Mediterranean identity is also visible in the history: the area was home to Mediterranean peoples (starting with the Phoenicians and then the ancient Romans). The Roman presence is clearly visible in the remains of the city of Baelo Claudia around twenty kilometres from Tarifa, today the best-preserved Roman urban site on the Iberian Peninsula. As Predrag Matvejević wrote in *Mediterranean: A Cultural Landscape*: 'Mediterraneanity is acquired, not inherited; it is a decision, not a privilege.'

SARDINIA, OUTPOST OF EUROPE

Another place on the very edge of Europe with a strange mixture of dialects and traditions is Carloforte, the island to the south-west of Sardinia, where they speak the Ligurian dialect, even though this is a completely different part of Italy. On 6 September 1995 the writer Sergio Atzeni died there at the age of just forty-three, swallowed up despite being an excellent swimmer by the same Mediterranean that he had so magnificently described. There are those like me who have visited Carloforte just to see the rock where he dived in and to which he clung for hours before the rescuers arrived – too late. Carloforte is one of those strange jokes of the Mediterranean, once again confirming what Matvejević argued, namely that 'Europe was conceived on the Mediterranean'. 'I am Sardinian and European,' said Atzeni, who described Cagliari as 'the outpost of Europe with the flavour of Africa and the Orient at the gates of the West, home to a dark race related to Hannibal, coveted by barefoot marauders, battered by every wind, imbued with every kind of perfume and stench and all manner of ingenuity and vice as well as a few virtues'.

In nearby Sant'Antioco is a place where you can savour the scents of a quintessential expression of the sea: the sea silk museum. Sea silk is a fabric made from *Pinna nobilis*, the largest bivalve in the Mediterranean, a native species now at risk of extinction. It is the only fabric in the world to come from the sea. And the only person now able to spin the thread is Chiara Vigo, a candidate for UNESCO intangible heritage status. I met Chiara Vigo a few years ago when I went to visit her at her museum, which is also her laboratory. I spent an entire day there, during which Vigo, a brusque but maternal character, explained to me that the process is very protracted: the tuft of fibres has to be soaked for twenty-five days in fresh water that is changed every three hours, then moistened with lemon juice to lighten the colour, before it is put into a secret mix of fifteen kinds of seaweed to make it elastic, then spun with a myrtle spindle. Sea silk does not deteriorate, is not attacked by insects, has excellent insulation properties and is thinner than a hair but a thousand times stronger. The sea silk museum is a place that encapsulates the smell of the Mediterranean.

THE JADE-GREEN SEA OF HOMER'S GREECE

Forget about the more familiar face of Greece for a moment, the white and blue of the Aegean and its land as dry as dust. On its Ionian shores Greece has different colours, different rhythms and different scents, deriving from the luxuriant vegetation. For Homer the smell of the sea was powerful, oppressive, sometimes almost irritating, contrasting with the scents of the vegetation – strawberry trees, heather and myrtles as well as cypresses, pines and olive trees – vegetation not so dissimilar to that described in the *Odyssey*, 'the sweet-smelling cypress', 'the fragrant olive'. This was Homer's Greece, even though its most eloquent champion in modern times was an Englishman, Gerald Durrell: 'grey-green olives; black cypresses; multi-coloured rocks of the sea-coast; and the sea smooth and opalescent, kingfisher-blue, jade-green'. In one of the best books written about this small corner of the Mediterranean, *My Family and Other Animals*, Durrell's description of his childhood in Corfu in the 1930s and 40s as part of an English family is told through the eyes of the future naturalist. The jagged mountains and rugged lanes with their white pebbles are perfect for motorbikes. Like the Durrells, my family also lived for a time in Greece, but on board a boat. If I think about the smell of Preveza, the town where we lived in the Epirus region of the Ionian coast, the first thing that comes to me is the scent of the eucalyptus trees. And then the smell of the Ionion Marine boatyard, one of the many yards where boats are lifted from the water and placed into steel cradles for the winter. In Greece boatyards are much cheaper than in many other places, so many Italian, German, French, Serbian, British and Dutch yacht owners opt to come here and overwinter their little craft. Starting in the autumn and the early months of winter, these places become miniature international communities peopled by pensioners from all over Europe, who live in their boats like caravans. The dominant smell is brine but also damp, condensation on the sheets, the smell of mould in the clothes and then the omnipresent smell of epoxy resin as well as the seaweed attached to the yachts' hulls. Donkeys pop up everywhere, and every so often a little goat makes an appearance as well. When you are hungry you can visit one of the tavernas inland to eat a *kokoretsi* (lamb's offal kebab) or a *paidakia* (lamb chop). The extraordinarily slow pace of the service, the tables with their plastic cloths, the smell of fried courgettes and the owner's – unfounded – worries about not having enough food for everyone make you think you have been transported back into one of Durrell's books.

MALTA AND THE QUINTESSENTIAL MEDITERRANEAN CITY

Jean-Claude Izzo was in love with the cities of the Mediterranean, which he regarded as 'a geography of possibilities for happiness', each of them with 'their narrow, tortuous streets, teeming with people'. Izzo, a writer from Marseilles, also contrasted 'the Mediterranean alternative' with its 'sea between the lands', to the Atlanticism of the

north. Scents of garlic and basil, aromas of almonds and mint, Barcelona, Naples, Genoa, Istanbul, Alexandria, Tangier, Valletta. All these cities share two things: their smells and the glimpses of the sea from the steeply inclined streets typical of maritime towns. The first time I walked through the narrow streets of Valletta, I glimpsed a little square of blue at the end of the narrow, dark street. You might be in Syracuse or Marseilles, but sooner or later in these cities you catch a glimpse of the sea. Valletta is perhaps the perfect mix of all this and even more. One after the other, Malta has been home, in turn, to the Phoenicians, the Greeks, the Romans, the Arabs, the Normans, the Aragonese, the Knights of Malta, the French and the British. The buildings in the city centre are embellished with Arab-style balconies called *gallariji*; the writing in the shops is in Maltese and English but also Italian (which until 1934 was the official language), while the most common names on the signs by far are Italian: Camilleri or Azzopardi. Corto Maltese,

the dashing pirate from the eponymous Italian comic books, was born and raised right here, with an Andalusian mother and an English father. From the smells in the cake shops you would swear you were in Sicily, but there are also *pastizzeriji*, little shops selling *pastizzi*, savoury pastries filled with meat or vegetables. Like the British, you drive on the left in Malta, the churches are Baroque, the homes on the outskirts are built in the cubic style of Arab cities. According to Fernand Braudel, some identified Malta as one of the first cradles of Mediterranean civilisation, even earlier than Crete, a hypothesis that is borne out by the megalithic temples scattered across Malta and Gozo that date back to 3200 BCE. The little statuettes of buxom women leave no doubt: people here venerated the mother goddess, the goddess of fertility. The smell of limestone, the aroma of oregano and the Mediterranean is all around. I am sure I came across Corto Maltese on the docks in Valletta. He was a little older but still handsome and redolent of the sea.

A Sea of Books

PAOLO LODIGIANI
Translated by Alan Thawley

I n a bid to understand an 'ancient' sea like the Mediterranean, in search of a balance between a past all too laden with history, a troubled present and a future yet to be built, directing your reading according to contemporary relevance will lead you astray. Inevitably you have to return to the origins and look back over three millennia of the development of Western civilisation in the place where it was born and nurtured.

The Mediterranean's literary debut was a stunning one, a genuine miracle. Even before the spread of writing, a sublime work emerged from its virgin waters, perfect like Aphrodite, who presented herself to the world in the splendour of

Navigator, designer of wooden boats, writer of technical manuals, nautical guides and books on the culture of the sea – including *Barche tradizionali italiane* ('Traditional Italian Boats', 1992) and *La barca nel mito* ('The Boat in Myth', 2006) – Paolo Lodigiani is also the owner of vintage and classic boats, a teacher and an advocate for the sport of sailing, who has opened sailing schools in Senegal and Bolivia.

her nudity, rising from the foam of that same sea. Faced with such a marvel, the only response is admiration, amazement and emotion. The *Odyssey* also gave rise to a character destined for a brilliant future, Odysseus, with his multifaceted ingenuity, a master of deception, a brave and prudent hero, a faithful husband but prone to distraction, a sailor who roved the seas. He is our ancestor, the quintessential *Homo mediterraneus*. We know nothing about the blind author **Homer**, if he actually existed, but he captures Odysseus' nuances and contradictions with an extraordinary level of psychological acuity.

Daniel Mendelsohn
AN ODYSSEY
William Collins, 2017

I can think of no better book than this to demonstrate, if ever there was any need, that the *Odyssey* remains relevant to the modern world. In the novel, an enjoyable and entertaining read, we see one of the aspects of Odysseus' character that has received less attention, namely his role as a father, aged by the years and the hardships he has endured, returning home after a long absence. A father who his now-adult son Telemachus has to get to know and learn to love. In parallel to the events recounted by Homer, we have the story of the protagonist, a professor of classical literature who teaches a course on the *Odyssey*. When his elderly father unexpectedly enrols, he challenges his son's opinions with his disconcerting observations. The pair end up boarding a ship for an ill-fated Mediterranean cruise heading for Ithaca. They never get there, offering further proof that, as the poet **Cavafy** teaches us, the journey is more important than the destination. In a touching work tempered by humour, Mendelsohn delves into the meanders of the eternal dialectic between fathers and sons and, using Homer as a guide, shows us that classical culture is not sterile erudition but material pulsating with life.

Odysseus represents a civilisation in its nascent state, which blossomed around a sea still home to deities, nymphs and mermen. He laps up the wonders he discovers with a child's amazement. This magical world was too beautiful to last, and the other great sailors of the classical epic poems lack Odysseus' enchanted gaze. Jason, the hero of the *Argonautica*, written by **Apollonius of Rhodes** five centuries after the *Odyssey*, also charts an erratic and adventurous course, visiting unknown lands and strange peoples. He has a splendid ship, which even boasts the gift of speech, and a highly skilled crew, and yet he shows no enthusiasm for his venture. He sails grudgingly, at the mercy of events, while his prudence is the fruit of indecision rather than cunning. Worse still is the pious Aeneas. He outperforms Odysseus as a captain – not only does he follow rational routes but he delivers almost all of his companions safely to their journey's end – but his interest lies in the destination, Rome, rather than the journey, which is little more than a bureaucratic encumbrance. The fact is that by **Virgil**'s time the Mediterranean had lost its magic; no one really believed in the divine beings populating its waters any longer. The serene pagan religiosity that permeated Homer's world gave way to a metaphysical anxiety, a desire for transcendence that paved the way for the disappearance of the gods who were so human and shared our mortal feelings, vices and weaknesses, offering the prospect of good news for humanity but bad news for the Mediterranean.

Claudius Rutilius Namatianus
DE REDITU SUO
Blue Bonnet, 2017
A short poem dating from the 5th century CE, unfinished and handed down to us incomplete. In spite of the evocative flashes of poetry, from a literary point of view the quality is not outstanding. So why should we read it? The reason is that, while there are many literary works produced during periods of decline, those representing civilisations that have already collapsed are rare and therefore interesting. The Mediterranean civilisations went through long declines during which life continued as before, sometimes even more enjoyably, amid languid pleasures that encouraged a flowering of the

arts and literature. At a certain point, however, the barbarians arrived and drew a line under all this with their destructive vitality. *De reditu suo* is a work from the period following this collapse. Namatianus, a wealthy bourgeois denizen of Rome, recounts a journey that, like Odysseus' voyage, represents a return. With no reason to stay, he leaves the capital, now at the mercy of barbarian raids, to return to Provence, the land where his roots lay. He sails all along the Tyrrhenian coast like a fugitive, in winter, on a leaden sea beneath a dark sky. Around him he sees the ruins of a world coming apart. On the islands of the Tuscan Archipelago he encounters the first communities of Christian monks and cannot come to terms with the fact that these madmen chose a life of sacrifice and penance over the pleasures and beauties of Imperial Rome. The poem is cut off before revealing the end of this sad voyage, leaving the reader with a bitter sensation and a warning that remains relevant to this day: while the decline of a civilisation can be strangely seductive, after the collapse only emptiness and squalor remain.

The great monotheistic religions emerged around the Mediterranean but were not enamoured of it. The Israelites showed a genuine aversion to it; in their exodus from Egypt, when they came across a sea in their path, they crossed it by walking on the seabed so as not to have to set foot in a boat. There aren't many references to boats in the Bible, the most notable being the ark cast adrift on the floodwaters sent by God as a punishment. With the rise of Christianity the Mediterranean entered an era in which it lost the power of speech. It no longer spoke to people's hearts and imagination. Without their gods its waters were no longer fertile sources of literary inspiration. The sea was transformed from a living myth into a metaphor for moral confusion in which only the boat of faith could lead people to a safe harbour. **Dante** made Ulysses (Odysseus) an immortal symbol and, despite putting him in hell, gave him a nobility of intent that perhaps Homer's character did not possess. But he was no longer a Mediterranean hero; his metaphysical adventure took place beyond the Pillars of Hercules in an unknown ocean. Two centuries later another distinguished son of the Mediterranean, Columbus, really did venture into the unknown in a bid to reach the Indies. Never did a navigational error bring such explosive consequences – excellent for Europe, disastrous for those he believed to be Indians and not good for the Mediterranean. Once the melting pot of civilisations, it found itself relegated to a corner of history and from then on was simply the quarrelsome courtyard of a building contested by powers whose interests lay elsewhere.

Unexpectedly, mass tourism exploded four centuries later. Up until the early 20th century only a few very rich eccentrics and the local children had been in the habit of bathing in the sea, but over the course of a few decades millions of people discovered how pleasurable this could be, and so began the peaceful seasonal invasion that brings much larger masses than were mobilised in all the invasions and migrations of centuries past to the Mediterranean's shores. The impacts on the landscape, the environment, the economy and society have been huge. There has also been a side effect, although it cannot be attributed to tourism alone. The world's perceptions of the Mediterranean changed as did, even more profoundly, the way the Mediterranean sees itself.

After centuries of marginalisation the Mediterranean once again finds itself at the centre, albeit of a secondary sector, and this has encouraged it to seek out its own identity and not just in the memory of the past.

Among the thinkers who have contributed the most to this search for identity are a historian and a novelist, both of them French and both born in the early years of the 20th century. The historian was **Fernand Braudel**, who, rather than an event or a period of history, placed a geographical area, the Mediterranean, at the heart of his work, redefining its role at the same time as revolutionising historiography.

Predrag Matvejević
MEDITERRANEAN:
A CULTURAL LANDSCAPE
University of California Press, 1999

'What is the Mediterranean?' wrote Braudel in UNESCO's *The Courier* magazine (December 1985). 'A thousand things at once. Not one landscape, but landscapes without number. Not one sea, but a succession of seas. Not one civilization, but a number of civilizations, superimposed one on top of the other ... All this is because the Mediterranean is a very ancient crossroads upon which, for thousands of years, everything has converged – men, beasts of burden, vehicles, merchandise, ships, ideas, religions and the arts of living.' These few lines of Braudel's definition are admirably developed in highly enjoyable style over more than three hundred pages in the Yugoslav writer Matvejević's *Mediterranean: A Cultural Landscape*. An erudite, unpredictable and curious companion, the author takes us with him on his meandering journey with no destination or itinerary, a pleasingly disorganised exploration of the history, traditions and nature of the Mediterranean. This is a sensory as well as a literary experience. We smell the acrid odour of the tar that is used to caulk the boats in Venetian boatyards and the scents of the spices unloaded on the docks. We hear the confused clamour of dialects on the harbourside stalls, share the boredom and languor of harbourmasters' offices in the Levantine ports, as well as the meticulous work of the scribes, bent over their parchments, who traced out the lines of ancient nautical maps. We savour the pleasure of sipping a coffee while lazily watching the bustle of life around us. In the background we can always make out the sparkling of the sun's rays on the waters of the Mediterranean. It is a strange, fascinating book, difficult to define. 'Breviary', its original title, is the most appropriate term to describe it, relating it to the small-format prayer books that people could carry with them and find the right words to praise and thank the Lord at all times. This is how Predrag's book should be used, with the difference here being that the prayers are in praise of a sea rather than a god.

Albert Camus is the most Mediterranean of the great 20th-century writers. He was born and raised in Algeria, a land he loved deeply, and after being forced to leave following the dramatic events of decolonisation, always felt like an exile. 'I grew up with the sea,' he wrote, 'and poverty for me was sumptuous. Then I lost the sea and found all luxuries grey.' Camus' love for the Mediterranean is simultaneously sensual and spiritual. He loved its beauty, the light and the sun but knew it was no idyllic world and that tragedy also formed a part of it. He regretted the loss of the Greek spirit, its taste for beauty, its sense of limits and proportion, which seemed to him to have been 'exiled' in post-war Europe, Greece's degenerate daughter. In his essays he lays the foundations for the 'southern thought' (*pensée de midi*) that he hoped, while harbouring no illusions, could be the Mediterranean's ideal contribution to the creation of a better future for humanity after the madness and horror of the first half of the century.

Franco Cassano
SOUTHERN THOUGHT
Fordham University Press, 2012

In this short collection of essays of admirable clarity, philosopher Franco Cassano develops the concept of southern thought, a way of thinking or, perhaps even better, a sensibility that is born out of the complicity between land and sea that is inherent in the Mediterranean. It develops when shore meets sea, and you discover that the world does not end but opens up to engagement with the other. The result is a dialectic between stability and change, between separation and coming together. While the land drives a consolidation of identity and fundamentalism, the sea prepares the mind for mobility and plurality, obliging us to be open to travel, to experience and accept diversity. In contrast to the single-track thinking imposed by an economistic and coldly rational vision, southern thought shies away from trenchant judgements, clear distinctions between what is good or evil, just or unjust, accepts contradictions and loves mediation. More than on abstract rationality, it is based on collaborative reasoning, valuing the complementarity and smoothing over oppositions rather than exacerbating them with the certainties of those who think they are always on the right side.

Today's world does not see southern thought as a successful formula, quite the opposite. Around the Mediterranean the persistence of wars, fanaticism and dictatorships, the tragedies of shipwrecks and migrant pushbacks, the devastation of landscape and environment, everything seems to disprove the practical effectiveness of this way of thinking, even in the very place where its roots lie. As a result it can resemble one of the many noble utopias that have emerged over the course of history before vanishing, defeated, without trace. The history of the Mediterranean contains examples of these but also ideas that have emerged from the bottom up, from the peripheries, that have been ignored or supressed but remained active under the radar for many years before ultimately prevailing over dominant ideologies that appeared invincible. So there are grounds for hope that southern thinking is a case in point and that one day these fundamental values of the Mediterranean will re-emerge, having seemingly been lost in the depths of its waters like the ancient marine deities. We need only add '*Inshallah*', as, with Mediterranean wisdom, the people of the southern and eastern coasts do when talking of the future – and with more of a philosophical angle than one of faith.

The Playlist

You can listen to this playlist at:
open.spotify.com/user/iperborea

INVERNOMUTO
Translated by Alan Thawley

Black Med is an archive in progress of sounds, music and sonic objects that Invernomuto began compiling in 2018 at the invitation of Manifesta12, a nomadic biennial that was being held that year in Palermo, the centre of the Mediterranean. Since then the project has developed along stratified, shape-shifting lines, through an online platform (blackmed.invernomuto. info), a book (*Black Med*, Humboldt Books, 2022) and a series of exhibitions and performances including the 58th Venice Biennale (2019), the Pompeii Archaeological Park (2021), Void (Derry, 2022) and OGR (Turin, 2022). Black Med has its origins in theoretical reflections on the Black Mediterranean, with reference to the research conducted by the academic Alessandra Di Maio. It sets out to intercept the sonic trajectories that run through the complex and stratified Mediterranean area, recording its constant movements and accommodating its interwoven events and narratives. The archive brings together elements that tell different stories and chart different diasporic paths; the selection is deliberately non-geographic and contains multiple voices and identities.

The playlist represents a small but significant taster of the Black Med archive, but above all, it sets out the approach adopted in compiling it, a task in part delegated to a network of people, artists and researchers. The itinerary begins with a minimalist suite by Franco Battiato, which imagines a luxuriant, pre-desert version of Egypt, before moving on to a 1959 composition by Halim El-Dabh, a prolific Cairo-based composer who was responsible for a series of pioneering sound and ethno-musicological experiments. This is followed by some vernacular examples of contemporary rap from the wider Arab world. The Mediterranean is not just physically explored but also imagined from afar by the Brazilian Tropicália artist Gal Costa as she celebrates the nomadic life of the Tuareg.

INVERNOMUTO — Moving images and sound are the channels of research favoured by Simone Bertuzzi and Simone Trabucchio, the duo who together make up Invernomuto. Invernomuto investigates subcultural universes in which the vernacular language is one way of approaching and appreciating oral cultures and contemporary mythologies, observed with a gaze that aspires to be cross-pollinated by it. Both artists also follow their own individual paths with their musical projects Palm Wine and STILL.

1
Franco Battiato
L'Egitto prima delle sabbie
1978

2
Halim El-Dabh
Leila Visitations Two
2001

3
Naar, Shayfeen, Hornet La Frappe
Babor
2019

4
Gal Costa
Tuareg
1969

5
Still
Banzina (Banzina riddim)
2017

6
Wizkid
Pakurumo
2011

7
Cheb Hasni
Chira Iy nabghiha
1991

8
PNL
Le monde ou rien
2015

9
Tony Esposito
Processione sul mare
1976

10
Nadah El Shazly
Palmyra
2017

11
Al Nather, Shabjdeed
Mtaktak
2019

12
Carl Gari, Abdullah Miniawy
Zyaj
2019

13
Zuli, Mado Sam, Abanob, Abyusif
Ana Ghayeb
2018

14
Hamid Baroudi
Caravan II Bagdad
1994

15
Mohammad Reza Mortazavi
Riding Time
2019

Digging Deeper

David Abulafia
*The Great Sea: A Human History
of the Mediterranean*
Oxford University Press, 2013
(USA) / Allen Lane, 2011 (UK)

Jeremy Black
A Brief History of the Mediterranean
Robinson, 2020

Caterina Bonvicini
The Year of Our Love
Other Press, 2021

Fernand Braudel
Memory and the Mediterranean
Knopf, 2001

Cyprian Broodbank
*The Making of the Middle Sea: A History
of the Mediterranean from the Beginning
to the Emergence of the Classical World*
Oxford University Press, 2013 (USA) /
Thames and Hudson, 2013 (UK)

Iain Chambers
*Mediterranean Crossings: The Politics
of an Interrupted Modernity*
Duke University Press, 2008

Bruce Clark
*Twice a Stranger: How Mass Expulsion
Forged Modern Greece and Turkey*
Granta, 2006

Omar El Akkad
What Strange Paradise
Knopf, 2021 (USA) / Picador, 2021 (UK)

Mathias Énard
Tell Them of Battles, Kings and Elephants
New Directions, 2018 (USA) /
Fitzcarraldo, 2018 (UK)

Davide Enia
*Notes on a Shipwreck: A Story
of Refugees, Borders, and Hope*
Other Press, 2019

Homer, Emily Wilson (tr.)
The Odyssey
W.W. Norton, 2018

Egidio Ivetic
*History of the Adriatic: A Sea
and Its Civilization*
Polity, 2022

Anja Kampmann
High as the Waters Rise
Catapult, 2020

Robert D. Kaplan
*Adriatic: A Concert of Civilizations
at the End of the Modern Age*
Random House, 2022

Emma-Jane Kirby
The Optician of Lampedusa
Allen Lane, 2016

Christopher Logue
War Music: An Account of Homer's Iliad
Farrar, Straus and Giroux, 2017 (USA) /
Faber and Faber, 2017 (UK)

Ċetta Mainwaring
*At Europe's Edge: Migration and
Crisis·in the Mediterranean*
Oxford University Press, 2019

Predrag Matvejević
Mediterranean: A Cultural Landscape
University of California Press, 1999

Jonathan Miles
*Once Upon a Time World: The Dark and
Sparkling Story of the French Riviera*
Pegasus Books, 2023 (USA) /
Atlantic Books, 2023 (UK)

Cees Nooteboom
533 Days
Yale University Press, 2022 (USA) /
MacLehose, 2021 (UK)

Christophe Picard / Nicholas Elliott (tr.)
*Sea of Caliphs: The Mediterranean
in the Medieval Islamic World*
Harvard University Press, 2018

Lorenza Pieri
Lesser Islands
Europa Editions, 2023

Nikolaj Schultz
Land Sickness
Polity, 2023

Elif Shafak
The Island of Missing Trees
Bloomsbury, 2021

Fabien Toulmé
Hakim's Odyssey (series)
Graphic Mundi, 2021–3

Tommy Wieringa / Sam Garrett (tr.)
The Death of Murat Idrissi
Scribe, 2019

Digging Deeper

Graphic design and art direction: Tomo Tomo
and Pietro Buffa

Photography: Rachel Cobb, Nick Hannes,
Laura León Gómez, André Liohn, Alessia Morellini,
Piero Percoco, Daniel Rodrigues, Tamara Saade

Photographic content curated by Prospekt Photographers
with Michela Mosca
Illustrations: Vincenzo Del Vecchio
Infographics and cartography: Propp

Managing editor (English-language edition): Simon Smith

Thanks to: Anna Basile, Chiara Comito, Ebru Değirmenci,
Marine Duval, Maddalena Giusto, Laura Grandi,
Zülfü Livaneli, Paolo Lodigiani, Gabi Martinez,
Tommaso Melilli, Valentina Pigmei, Sabine Réthoré,
Cristina Vezzaro

The opinions expressed in this publication are those of the
authors and do not purport to reflect the views and opinions
of the publishers. All content not specifically credited was
written by *The Passenger*.

http://europaeditions.com/thepassenger
http://europaeditions.co.uk/thepassenger
#ThePassengerMag

The Passenger – Mediterranean
© Iperborea S.r.l., Milan, and Europa Editions, 2024

Translators: French — Sam Taylor; German — Stephen
Smithson; Italian — Eleanor Chapman ('Shipwreck'),
Alan Thawley ('The Cicadas and the Breath of the World',
'The Geopolitics Corner', 'An Olfactory Map', 'An Ocean
of Books', 'The Playlist', editorial, standfirsts, sidebars,
captions); Turkish — Kate Ferguson

Translations © Iperborea S.r.l., Milan, and Europa Editions,
2024, except 'The Liquid Road' © Sam Taylor, 2020

ISBN 9781787704794

Printed on Munken Pure thanks to the support of Arctic Paper

Printed by ELCOGRAF S.p.A., Verona, Italy